Elements

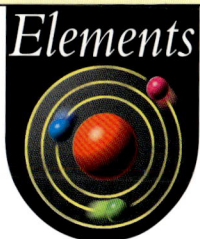

Francium
to Polonium

Atlantic Europe Publishing

How to use this set

The *Elements* set has been carefully developed to help you understand the chemistry of the elements. Volumes 1 to 15 provide an in-depth look at the 32 best-known elements.

Volumes 16 to 18 outline the properties, uses, discovery, technology, geology and biology of all the elements known up to 118. There is also a key facts table of comparative data for each element.

Volumes 16 to 18 present the elements in alphabetical order, with the full name of the element and its symbol (e.g. americium – Am). Frequently, an element's symbol derives from a different word than its common name. For instance, Ag (from the Latin word *argentum*) is the symbol for silver. To help you find these elements by symbol, the symbols appear alphabetically at the tops of appropriate pages. For example, Ag appears on the page for aluminium and points you to silver: Ag *see* Silver.

At the back of each volume is a glossary and an index to all 18 volumes in the set.

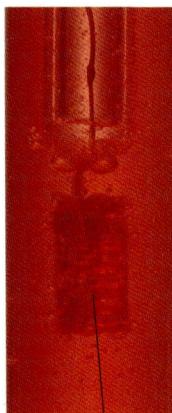

The relatively low reactivity of platinum makes it suitable for electrodes.

Iodine has a characteristic violet colour.

Author
Brian Knapp, BSc, PhD
Project consultant
Keith B. Walshaw, MA, BSc, DPhil
Art Director
Duncan McCrae, BSc
Editors
Mary Sanders, BSc, and Gillian Gatehouse
Special photography
Ian Gledhill
Illustrations
David Woodroffe
Designed and produced by
EARTHSCAPE EDITIONS
Reproduced in Malaysia by
Global Colour Separation
Printed in Hong Kong by
Wing King Tong Company Ltd

First published in 2002 by
Atlantic Europe Publishing Company Limited,
Greys Court Farm, Greys Court,
Henley-on-Thames, Oxon RG9 4PG, UK

Elements
Volume 17: *Francium to Polonium*
A CIP record for this book is available from the British Library

ISBN 1-86214-064-2

Acknowledgments
The publishers would like to thank the following for their kind help and advice: *British Petroleum International* and *UKAEA Technology.*

Picture credits
All photographs are from the **Earthscape Editions** photolibrary except the following:
(c=centre t=top b=bottom l=left r=right)
British Petroleum International 9cl; **NASA** 1, 14bl, 15tc; **UKAEA Technology** 25t; **ZEFA** 20tl.

Title page: Hydrogen is the most abundant element in the universe. It is the fuel that burns in a star such as our Sun, creating helium and producing temperatures of 10,000,000°C.

This product is manufactured from sustainable managed forests.
For every tree cut down at least one more is planted.

The demonstrations described or illustrated in this book are not for replication. The Publisher cannot accept any responsibility for any accidents or injuries that may result from conducting the experiments described or illustrated in this book.

Contents

Francium (Fr)   4
Gadolinium (Gd)   5
Gallium (Ga)   6
Germanium (Ge)   7
Gold (Au)   8
Hafnium (Hf)   10
Hassium (Hs)   11
Helium (He)   12
Holmium (Ho)   13
Hydrogen (H)   14
Indium (In)   16
Iodine (I)   17
Iridium (Ir)   18
Iron (Fe)   19
Krypton (Kr)   21
Lanthanum (La)   22
Lawrencium (Lr)   23
Lead (Pb)   24
Lithium (Li)   26
Lutetium (Lu)   27
Magnesium (Mg)   28
Manganese (Mn)   30
Meitnerium (Mt)   31
Mendelevium (Md)   32
Mercury (Hg)   33
Molybdenum (Mo)   35
Neodymium (Nd)   36
Neon (Ne)   37
Neptunium (Np)   38
Nickel (Ni)   39
Niobium (Nb)   40
Nitrogen (N)   41
Nobelium (No)   43
Osmium (Os)   44
Oxygen (O)   45
Palladium (Pd)   48
Phosphorus (P)   49
Platinum (Pt)   51
Plutonium (Pu)   52
Polonium (Po)   53
The Periodic Table   54
Understanding equations   56
Set Index   58

Francium (Fr)

Element 87. Francium is the heaviest and most reactive alkali metal in group 1 in the Periodic Table.

It is a radioactive metal that only occurs in the most minute quantities. It is the most unstable of the first 101 elements, with a half-life of 22 minutes. Its properties are very similar to those of cesium.

Discovery

Marguerite Perey of the Curie Institute in Paris discovered francium in 1939. However, it has never been isolated as the pure element. Because it is so radioactive, it quickly decays to other elements. The longest lived isotope, francium-223, has a half-life of 22 minutes. It is the only isotope of francium that occurs in nature.

Technology

It has no uses. It can be produced artificially by bombarding thorium with protons.

Geology

Natural francium is present in only the minutest of quantities in nature, perhaps less than 30g in the entire Earth's crust at any one time. It is produced by the disintegration of actinium. It is found in uranium minerals.

Biology

As a radioactive element it is theoretically harmful but it is produced only in tiny quantities.

Key facts...
Name: francium
Symbol: Fr
Atomic number: 87
Atomic weight: 223
Position in Periodic Table: group 1 (1) (alkali metal); period 7
State at room temperature: solid
Colour: metallic
Density: n/a
Melting point: 27°C
Boiling point: 677°C
Origin of name: named after France
Shell pattern of electrons: 2–8–18–32–18–8–1

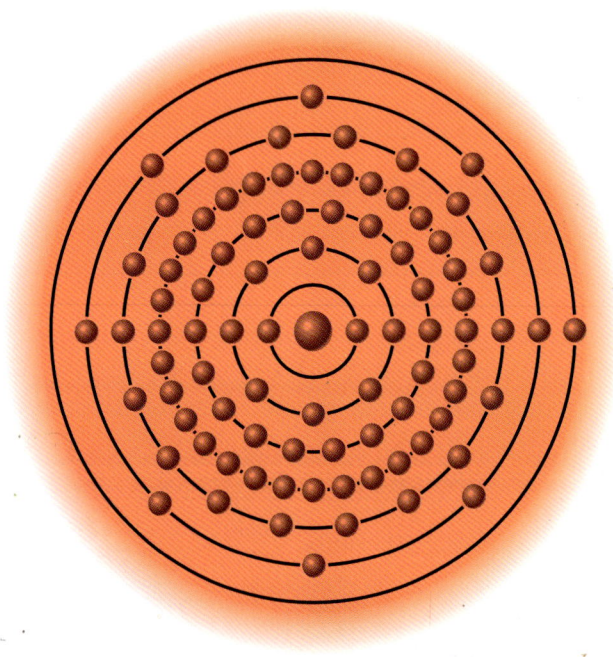

Gadolinium (Gd)

Element 64. A silvery-white and easily bent rare-earth metal (lanthanide) in the Periodic Table. It was named after John Gadolin, a Finnish chemist.

Gadolinium is easily worked, but it is not very reactive in dry air; it quickly tarnishes in damp air. The oxide forms a loose film, which readily flakes or chips off, exposing more surface to oxidation. It is strongly magnetic. It reacts slowly with water but is soluble in dilute acids.

Discovery

Discovered by Jean-Charles Galinard de Marignac and Paul-Émile Lecoq de Boisbaudran in Switzerland 1880 as new spectral lines in the mineral gadolinite.

Technology

Gadolinium is used for electronic components such as capacitors and for making phosphors on TV tubes. It also goes into alloys, CDs and control rods in nuclear reactors. Synthetic gadolinium–yttrium garnets are used for generating the microwaves in some microwave ovens.

Geology

Not found as a native element, but in gadolinite and monazite ores.

Biology

It does not occur in the body and has no biological role. It is not thought to be harmful.

Key facts...
Name: gadolinium
Symbol: Gd
Atomic number: 64
Atomic weight: 157.25
Position in Periodic Table: inner transition metal; period 6 (lanthanide series)
State at room temperature: solid
Colour: silvery-white
Density of solid: 7.90 g/cc
Melting point: 1,311°C
Boiling point: 3,233°C
Origin of name: named after the Finnish chemist Johan Gadolin
Shell pattern of electrons: 2–8–18–25–9–2

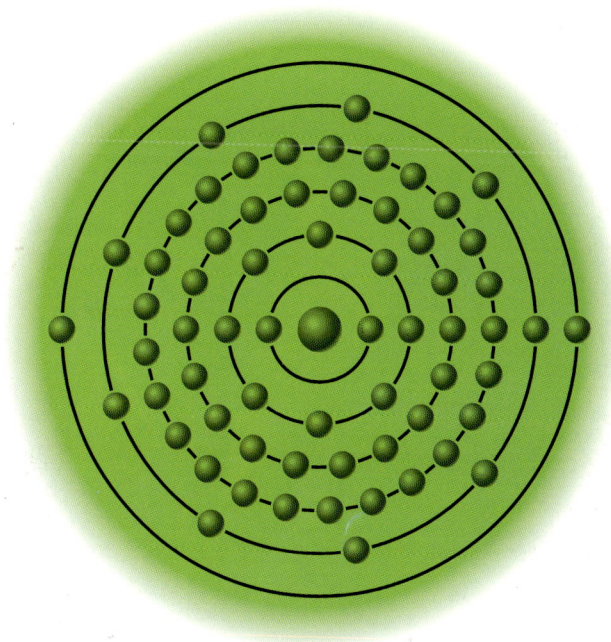

Gallium (Ga)

Element 31. Gallium is a rare silvery-white metal in the boron group, which is group 3 in the Periodic Table. The solid metal is brittle and breaks with a conchoidal fracture like glass. The metal expands on solidifying and has a melting point just above room temperature. Some gallium compounds emit light when an electric current passes through them.

Discovery

Gallium was discovered by Paul-Émile Lecoq de Boisbaudran in 1875 as an impurity in zinc blende (sulphide).

Technology

Its low melting point and high boiling point make it possible to use it in high-temperature thermometers. Gallium arsenide goes into making LEDs (light-emitting diodes). It is also used for doping semi-conductors. It makes a brilliant mirror when painted on glass. Ninety tonnes of gallium in large tanks (three years of world production) are used to detect solar neutrinos.

Geology

Gallium is not found as a native element. It is normally recovered as a by-product of other ores.

Biology

It has no biological role.

Key facts...
Name: gallium
Symbol: Ga
Atomic number: 31
Atomic weight: 69.72
Position in Periodic Table: group 3 (13) (boron group); period 4
State at room temperature: solid
Colour: silvery-white
Density of solid: 5.90 g/cc
Melting point: 29.76°C
Boiling point: 2,403°C
Origin of name: from the Latin word *Gallia*, meaning France
Shell pattern of electrons: 2–8–18–3

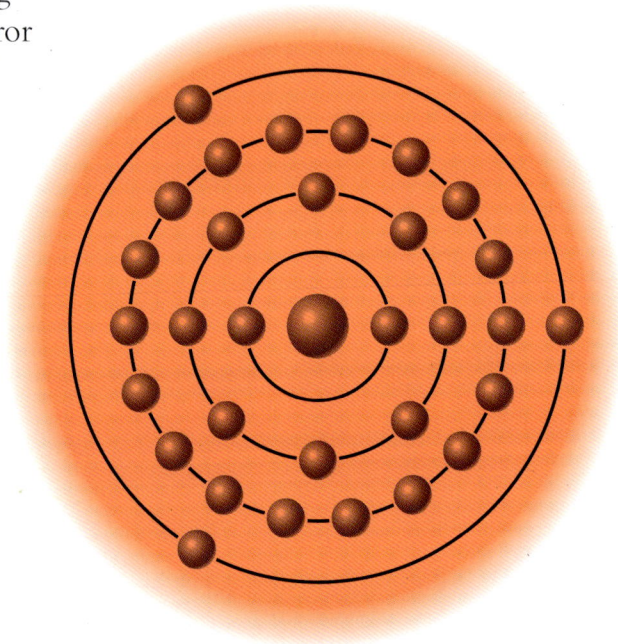

Germanium (Ge)

Element 32. Germanium, a rare, brittle, silvery-grey metalloid, is in group 4 (the carbon group) in the Periodic Table. Germanium does not readily react with air and so remains lustrous.

Discovery

It was predicted by Dmitri Ivanovich Mendeleev in 1871 and called ekasilicon. It was actually discovered by Clemens Winkler, a German chemist, in 1886.

Technology

Germanium is important as a semi-conductor. It can be doped with arsenic, gallium and other elements to make part of a microprocessor. It is a phosphor in fluorescent lamps and also an alloying agent. The high refractive index of germanium oxide makes it suitable for use in some high-quality wide-angle and microscope lenses. It is also a catalyst.

Geology

Germanium is not found in native form but in germanite, which contains 8% of the element, in argyrodite, a sulphide of germanium and silver, in some zinc ores and in coal. It is obtained from the dusts of zinc smelters and from combustion by-products of coal.

Biology

Germanium does not occur naturally in the body, but compounds are non-toxic to people while being poisonous to some bacteria. That makes them potentially valuable as medicines.

Key facts...

Name: germanium
Symbol: Ge
Atomic number: 32
Atomic weight: 72.59
Position in Periodic Table: group 4 (14) (carbon group); period 4
State at room temperature: solid
Colour: silvery-grey
Density of solid: 5.32 g/cc
Melting point: 937°C
Boiling point: 2,830°C
Origin of name: from the Latin word *Germania*, meaning Germany
Shell pattern of electrons: 2–8–18–4

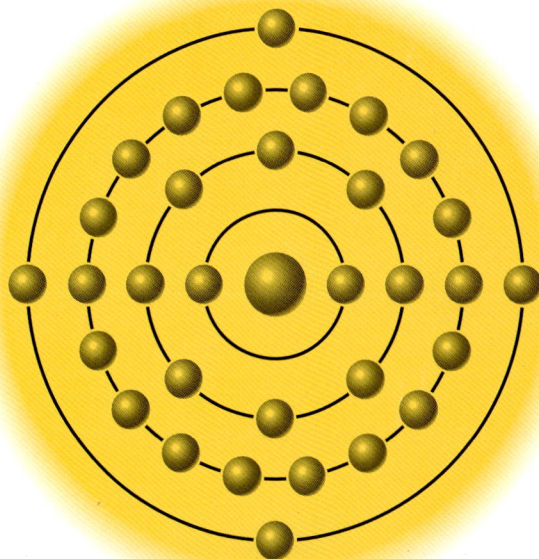

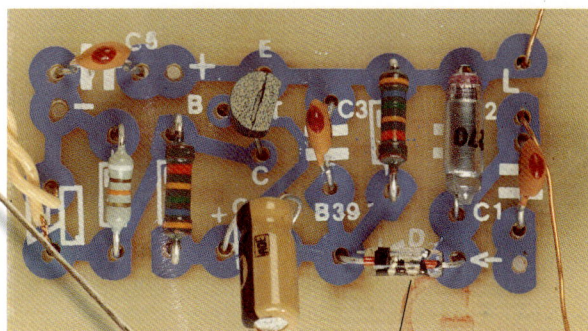

This germanium diode forms part of a circuit.

Gold (Au)

Element 79. Gold is a dense, heavy, shiny, yellow precious metal and one of the transition metals in the Periodic Table.

Gold is soft and easily shaped – even making the thin sheets called gold leaf. One gram (ounce) of gold can be beaten to a sheet of gold that covers 15 sq m (300 sq ft). It does not tarnish or corrode.

Its traditional role in coins and low reactivity have made it the one material that can be used worldwide instead of money.

Gold is a good conductor of heat and electricity, and it is plated over switch contacts and other places where it is important that no corrosion occurs. Gold has also long been used for tooth fillings, partly because it doesn't corrode, and partly for its decorative effect.

Key facts...

Name: gold
Symbol: Au
Atomic number: 79
Atomic weight: 196.96
Position in Periodic Table: transition metal, group (11) (copper group; coinage metal); period 6
State at room temperature: solid
Colour: yellow-metallic
Density of solid: 19.3
Melting point: 1,063°C
Boiling point: 2,966°C
Origin of name: from the Anglo-Saxon word *gold*; the symbol Au is from the Latin word *aurum*, meaning gold.
Shell pattern of electrons: 2–8–18–32–18–1

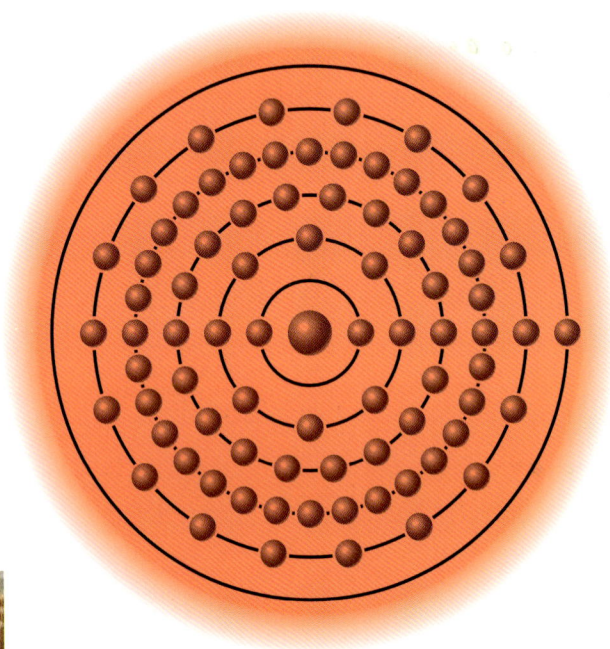

▲ Gold is a very good electrical conductor and does not develop an insulating oxide layer (as happens, for example, with aluminium). However it is expensive and so is used sparingly or in a thin skin for important electrical components, such as these gold-plated contacts.

Discovery

Gold has been known since ancient times.

Technology

Gold does not stand up to continual handling and, to make it useful, it is alloyed with other metals. Most gold that goes into jewellery is an alloy with silver, copper and zinc. White gold is 70% silver. Gold alloys are measured in 24ths, or carats – 24-carat gold is pure gold.

Geology

It is found widely in pure native form in veins close to ancient volcanoes. It also appears in rivers, where it was traditionally recovered by panning. Most of the river gold (called placer gold) comes in small pieces, but sometimes large nuggets do occur.

The fact that it could be found so easily, and that it is soft and does

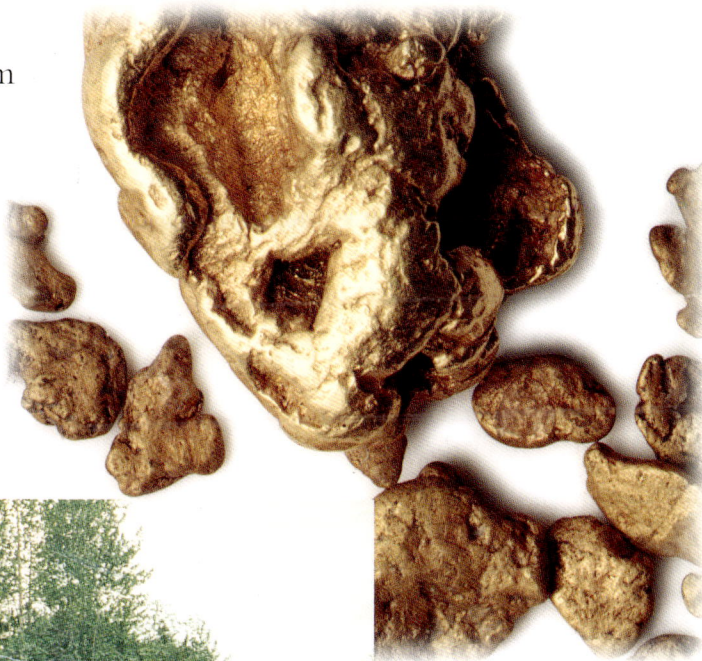

▲ A gold nugget and flakes. Each flake is about 3mm long.

◀ Panning for gold on the Klondike River in Canada.

▼ A Krugerrand, one of the world's most famous gold coins.

not corrode, explains why it was one of the first metals ever used by people. However, all the gold in the world that has so far been refined would still only make up a cube with a 20m/60ft side.

Gold is now extracted from ores in which the gold content is tiny, and the huge volumes crushed can cause wide environmental damage.

Biology

Gold is not naturally found in the body, but it has been used to treat rheumatoid arthritis.

For more on gold, see Volume 5: Copper, Silver, and Gold in the *Elements* set.

Hafnium (Hf)

Element 72. A silvery, soft, bendable metal belonging to the transition metals in the Periodic Table. Hafnium is very similar to zirconium in properties, and it is difficult to separate the two elements. Hafnium is very corrosion resistant. It is not especially rare, being 45th in order of abundance in the Earth's crust.

It is an easily shaped metal with a brilliant silvery lustre.

Discovery

It was discovered by Dirk Coster and George Charles de Hevesy in 1923 in Copenhagen, Denmark. It was named after *Hafinia*, which is the Latin name for Copenhagen.

Technology

Hafnium absorbs neutrons and goes into control rods in nuclear reactors. An alloy of tantalum, hafnium and carbon has a very high melting point (4,215°C) and holds other materials that are to be melted. For example, it helps in the manufacture of tungsten filaments. Because of its high melting point and corrosion resistance it is also a structural material in nuclear power plants and nuclear submarines.

Geology

Hafnium is not found as a native element, but occurs mainly in zirconium minerals, where it makes up about 2% of the mineral. Alvite is a hafnium silicate mineral.

Biology

Hafnium is not found in living things and is not especially hazardous.

Key facts...
Name: hafnium
Symbol: Hf
Atomic number: 72
Atomic weight: 178.49
Position in Periodic Table: transition metal, group (4) (titanium group); period 6
State at room temperature: solid
Colour: silvery
Density of solid: 13.31 g/cc
Melting point: 2,227°C
Boiling point: 4,603°C
Origin of name: after the Latin name for the city of Copenhagen (*Hafnia*)
Shell pattern of electrons: 2–8–18–32–10–2

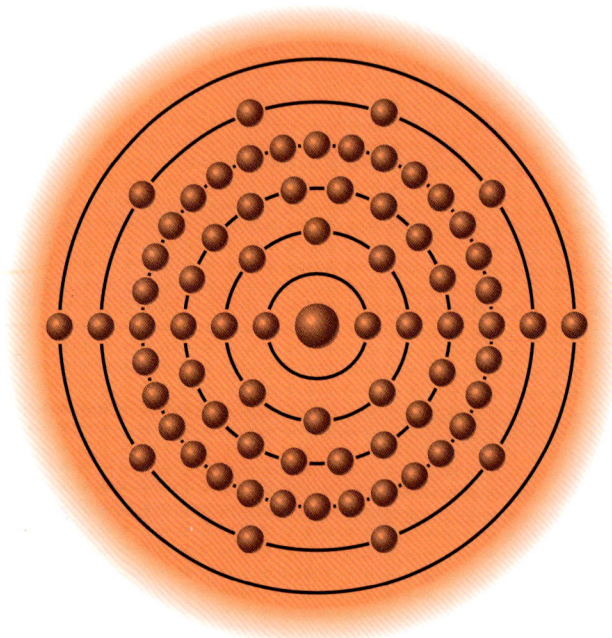

Hassium (Hs)

Element 108. Also formerly called unniloctium (Uno). It is an artificial radioactive element belonging to the transition metals in the Periodic Table. Hassium comes from the Latin word *Hassias* which means Hessen, a state in Germany.

Hassium has properties similar to osmium. Only a few atoms have ever been made in a nuclear reactor. Hassium decays very quickly as it gives out alpha particles.

Discovery

It was discovered in 1984 by West German researchers Peter Armbruster, Gottfried Münzenber and others at the Institute for Heavy Ion Research.

Technology

It has not yet been used for anything.

Geology

It is not found naturally.

Biology

It has no use in living things. Because it is a radioactive element, it would be potentially harmful if it were ever produced in significant quantities.

Key facts...
Name: hassium
Symbol: Hs
Atomic number: 108
Atomic weight: 265
Position in Periodic Table: transition metal, group (8) (iron group); period 7
State at room temperature: solid
Colour: unknown
Density: n/a
Melting point: n/a
Boiling point: n/a
Origin of name: from the Latin word *Hassias*, meaning Hessen, a state in Germany.
Shell pattern of electrons: 2–8–18–32–32–14–2

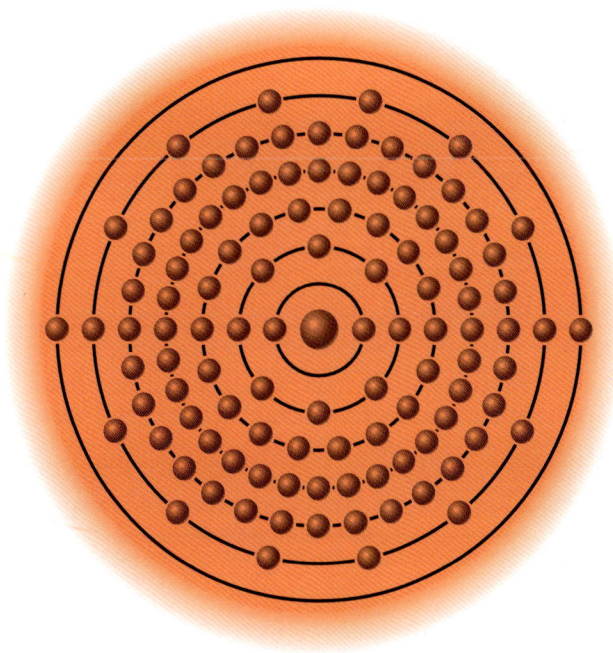

Helium (He)

Element 2. Helium is an inert (unreactive), colourless, and odourless gas in group 8 (the noble gases) in the Periodic Table. It is the second most abundant element, the second lightest (after hydrogen) in the universe and is very common in the hotter stars.

Helium is too light to be common in our atmosphere, although it is found combined with natural gas. Helium is obtained by liquefying natural gas. The helium is the last component to liquefy. Helium never becomes a solid under ordinary air pressure. Very cold helium (below −270.8°C) is sometimes called the fourth state of matter because it behaves so oddly. For example, it suddenly changes from being an insulator to a superconductor of electricity.

Discovery

Helium was discovered by the French astronomer Pierre Janssen in 1868 as a yellow line when looking at the light given out by the Sun. That is how the element got its name.

Technology

Helium is used in balloons and as an inert gas when there would otherwise be a risk of explosion with the lighter gas hydrogen. It is put into gas cylinders for divers, used to inflate some aircraft tyres, and to provide an inert atmosphere for delicate laboratory experiments, such as for growing crystals.

For more on helium, see Volume 1: Hydrogen and the Noble Gases in the Elements set.

Key facts...
Name: helium
Symbol: He
Atomic number: 2
Atomic weight: 4.00
Position in Periodic Table: group 8 (18) (noble gases); period 1
State at room temperature: gas
Colour: colourless
Density of gas at 20°C: 0.117 g/cc
Melting point: none (at atmospheric pressure); −272°C (only under pressure)
Boiling point: −269°C
Origin of name: named from the Greek *helios*, meaning the Sun
Shell pattern of electrons: 2

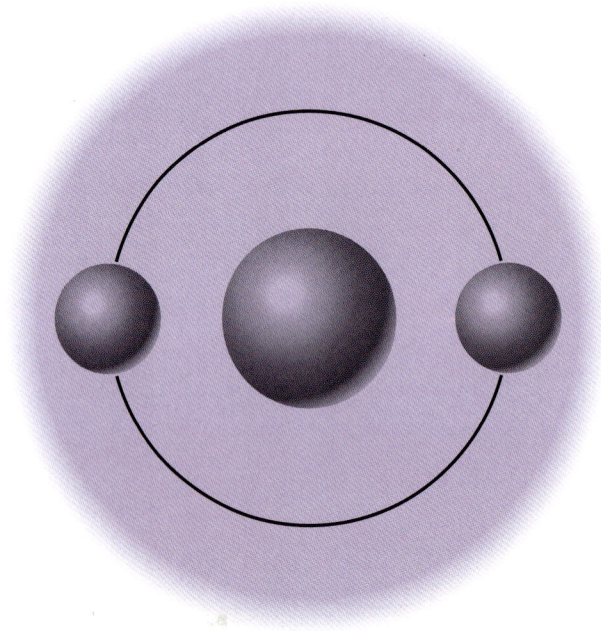

Geology

The helium that occurs on the Earth is a result of radioactive decay. It is normally isolated from natural gas mixtures, where concentrations can be as high as 7%.

Biology

Helium is less soluble in blood than nitrogen is and comes out of the blood more easily than nitrogen. It is often

Holmium (Ho)

Element 67. It is a rare-earth metal (lanthanide) in the Periodic Table.

It is soft and easily worked. It is highly magnetic and only reacts in air slowly, so that it does not tarnish readily.

Discovery

It was first identified in Stockholm in 1879 by the Swedish chemist T. Cleve.

Technology

It has few uses but is sometimes used in alloys.

Geology

Never found as a native element, but in monazite and gadolinite ores.

Biology

Holmium does not occur in living things.

> **Key facts...**
> **Name:** holmium
> **Symbol:** Ho
> **Atomic number:** 67
> **Atomic weight:** 164.9
> **Position in Periodic Table:** inner transition metal; period 6 (lanthanide series)
> **State at room temperature:** solid
> **Colour:** silvery-white
> **Density of solid:** 8.78 g/cc
> **Melting point:** 1,470°C
> **Boiling point:** 2,720°C
> **Origin of name:** named after *Holmia*, the Latin name for the city of Stockholm
> **Shell pattern of electrons:** 2–8–18–29–8–2

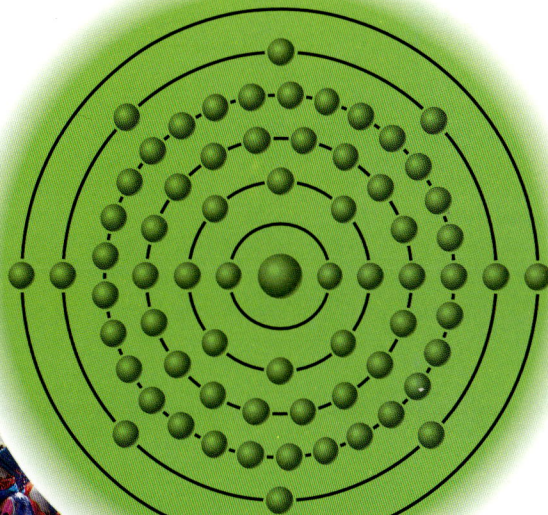

used in mixtures with oxygen for diving cylinders and prevents the 'bends'. Speaking after breathing an atmosphere rich in helium results in a squeaky voice. That is the way deep-sea divers are heard speaking because their air cylinders are helium-rich.

▶ Helium is used to fill party balloons and modern airships because it is safer than using hydrogen. It has almost the same lifting power as hydrogen, but cannot catch fire. Of all the helium produced, 10% is used for lifting.

Hydrogen (H)

Element 1. Hydrogen is the most common element in the universe. It has properties similar to those elements in groups 1 and 7, but it has been assigned to group 1 in the Periodic Table.

Hydrogen accounts for about 87% of all matter in the universe. It is the lightest gas known. Because it is so light, hydrogen is rare in the Earth's atmosphere. Hydrogen is, however, abundant in compounds – for example, it makes up just over a tenth of the mass of sea water.

Hydrogen is a colourless, odourless, tasteless and flammable gas. It is the simplest of all elements, having just one proton in its nucleus and one electron.

Hydrogen is easily made in the laboratory by reacting an acid with a metal. The gas given off is hydrogen. Hydrogen is produced commercially by reacting superheated steam with coke.

The isotope known as heavy water is deuterium (^{2}H, or D). Another isotope, tritium, is radioactive. It is used in the production of a hydrogen bomb.

▶ Hydrogen is the most abundant element in the universe. It is the fuel that burns in a star, creating helium and producing temperatures of 10,000,000°C.

Key facts...
Name: hydrogen
Symbol: H
Atomic number: 1
Atomic weight: 1.01
Position in Periodic Table: group 1 (1); period 1
State at room temperature: gas
Colour: colourless
Density of gas at 20°C: 0.083 g/l
Melting point: –259°C
Boiling point: –253°C
Origin of name: from the Greek words *hydro* (water) and *gen* (to make), meaning maker of water
Shell pattern of electrons: 1

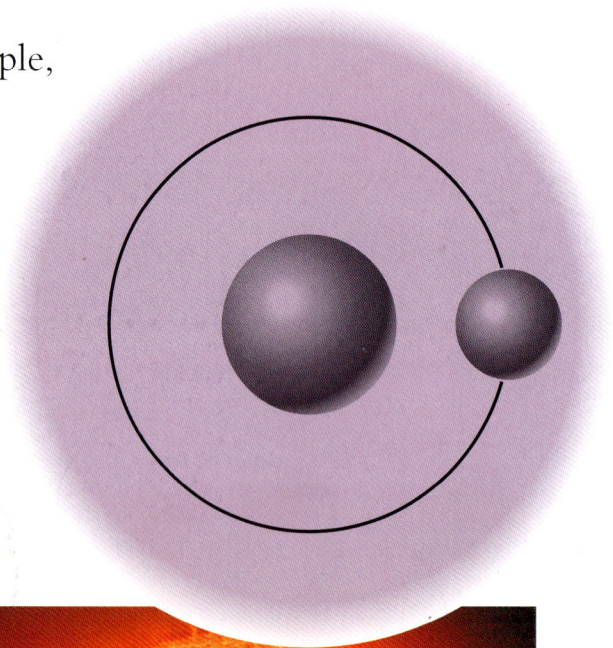

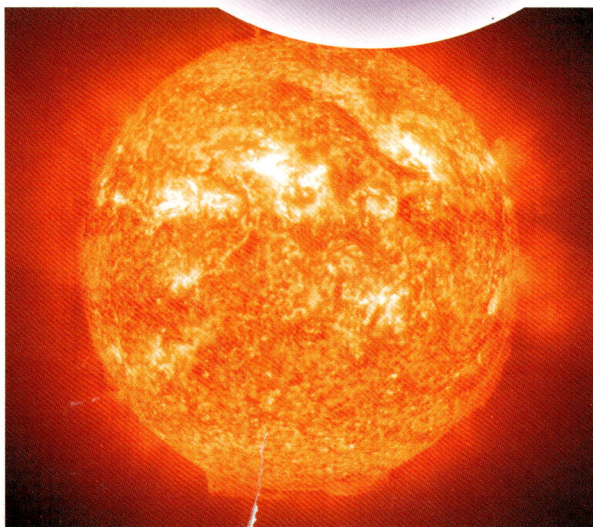

Discovery

English chemist Robert Boyle did experiments during the later 17th century with metals and acids that released hydrogen gas. However, hydrogen was identified as an element by English chemist Henry Cavendish in 1766. At that time it was called inflammable air from metals or phlogiston. The name hydrogen was given by French chemist Antoine-Laurent Lavoisier from the Greek meaning 'maker of water'.

Deuterium gas ($^2H_2$, or D_2), an isotope of hydrogen, was discovered in 1931 by Harold Urey in the United States.

Technology

Hydrogen gas is used to make many chemicals, including ammonia (which then goes into fertilisers using the Haber process). It is also used in some food, such as margarine. Hydrogen gas lifted hydrogen balloons, but its flammability caused problems for airships. Disasters such as the Hindenburg crash limited this application. It is a common rocket fuel and is used in fuel cells for making electricity. It is also involved in reducing metal ores. Liquid hydrogen aids low-temperature experiments (cryogenics) because its melting point is so close to absolute zero.

▲ A space shuttle taking off. The brown tank underneath the space shuttle contains liquid oxygen and hydrogen fuel.

Geology

Hydrogen is found in water and in a wide range of minerals in the Earth's crust. Hydrogen is the most common element in all stars, including our Sun, and is the primary source of their fuel through the fusion of hydrogen nuclei to make helium. Hydrogen is also very common on Jupiter (whose core may contain solid metallic hydrogen).

Biology

Hydrogen is part of all living things and is essential to all life. Every form of organic matter contains hydrogen.

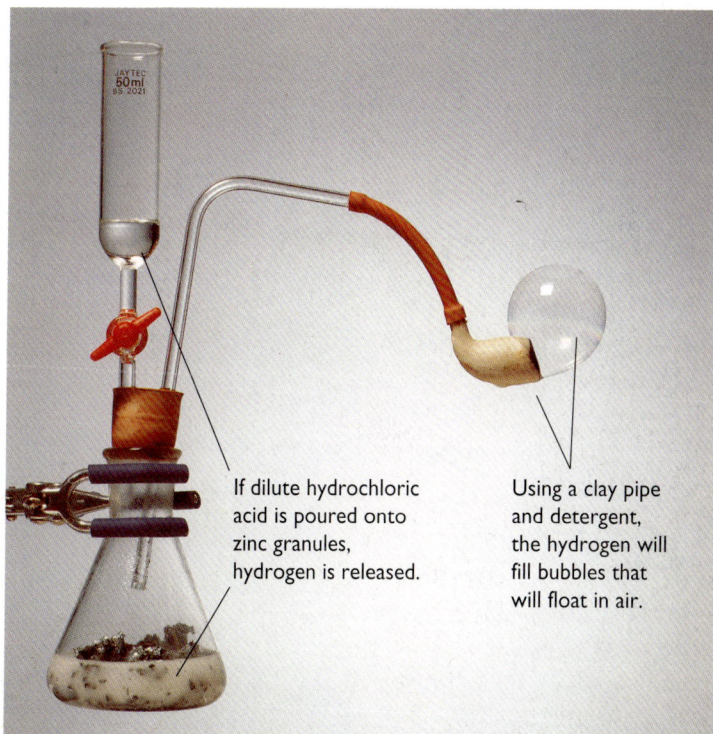

If dilute hydrochloric acid is poured onto zinc granules, hydrogen is released.

Using a clay pipe and detergent, the hydrogen will fill bubbles that will float in air.

▲ Hydrogen is the simplest and lightest atom of any element. Hydrogen gas is so light that the molecules can easily escape from the Earth's gravitational field, and so hydrogen is rarely found uncombined on Earth.

For more on hydrogen, see Volume 1: Hydrogen and the Noble Gases in the *Elements* set.

Indium (In)

Element 49. A rare silvery-white metal belonging to group 3 (the boron group) in the Periodic Table.

It is very soft and can easily be made to change shape. Pure indium 'screams' when it is bent. Indium will wet glass.

Discovery

Discovered in Germany in 1863 by Ferdinand Reich and Theodor Richter, using an instrument called a spectrometer, which analyses the unique range of colour given off by each element.

Technology

Indium is used in making electronic components such as transistors, rectifiers, thermistors, and photoconductors. It is also used in low-melting-point alloys. An alloy of 24% indium and 76% gallium is liquid at room temperature. It is also part of engine bearings to help oil stick to metal. Hermetic seals between glass and other materials can be made from it. Indium can be plated onto metal, and it will evaporate and then condense on glass, producing highly reflective mirrors. Such mirrors resist corrosion better than silver.

Geology

Indium is not found as the native element; it mainly occurs in iron, lead, copper and zinc ores. Indium is therefore recovered as a by-product of refining these more common metals. Indium is as abundant as silver, being 63rd most common of the elements in the Earth's surface rocks.

Biology

Indium is not found in living things but is not thought to be especially harmful.

Key facts...	
Name: indium	
Symbol: In	
Atomic number: 49	
Atomic weight: 114.82	
Position in Periodic Table: group 3 (13) (boron group); period 5	
State at room temperature: solid	
Colour: silvery-white	
Density of solid: 7.31 g/cc	
Melting point: 156.6°C	
Boiling point: 2,080°C	
Origin of name: named after the indigo-coloured line in its atomic spectrum	
Shell pattern of electrons: 2–8–18–18–3	

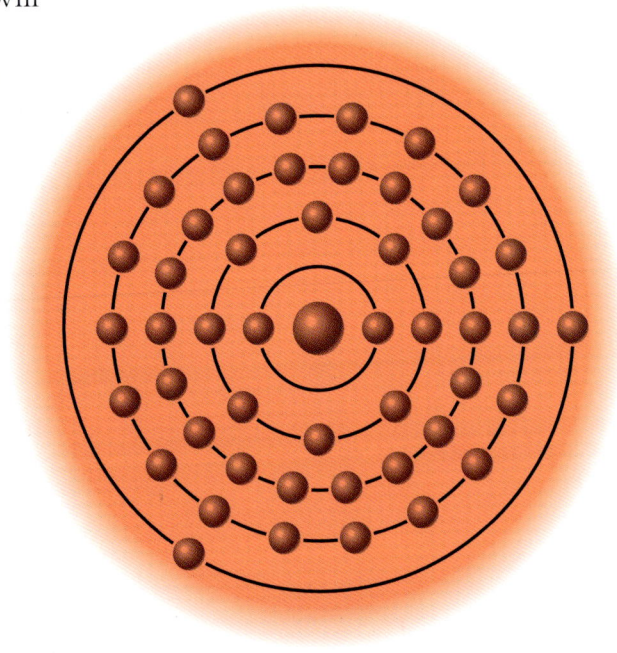

Iodine (I)

Element 53. Iodine is a violet-coloured nonmetallic element and one of the halogens in group 7 in the Periodic Table. Although it is the least reactive of the common halogens, it is still very reactive and forms compounds with most other elements.

Its compounds can be processed to make pure, dark violet crystals. At room temperature solid iodine turns into a vapour (it sublimes) to produce an unpleasantly irritating violet-coloured vapour.

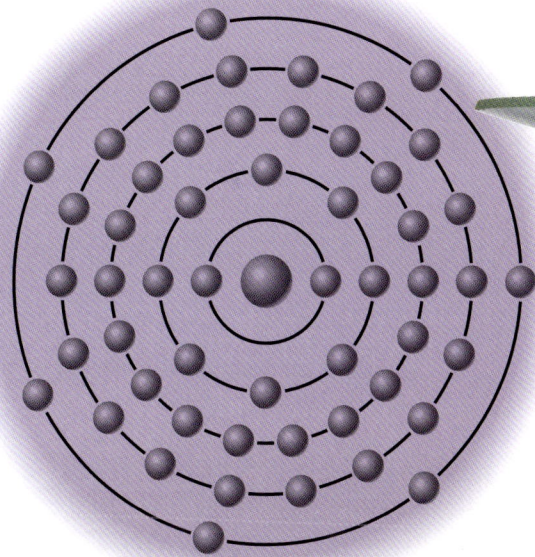

Key facts...
Name: iodine
Symbol: I
Atomic number: 53
Atomic weight: 126.90
Position in Periodic Table: group 7 (17) (halogens); period 5
State at room temperature: solid
Colour: violet
Density of solid: 4.93 g/cc
Melting point: 113.7°C
Boiling point: 184.3°C
Origin of name: from the Greek word *iodes*, meaning violet
Shell pattern of electrons: 2–8–18–18–7

Discovery

It was discovered in seaweed by Bernard Courtois in France in 1811.

Technology

It is used in medicine (a dilute solution of iodine in alcohol is called tincture of iodine and is applied as an antiseptic), in photography, and in colour dyes.

Geology

Iodine does not occur as a native element. It is found in sea water and accumulates in seaweeds. It is also found in some evaporite deposits in association with other salts and is sometimes recovered from salt wells.

Biology

Iodine is one of the essential nutrients in the body. Lack of iodine causes thyroid problems. To ensure that people get enough of it, iodine is added to most table salt. A solution of iodine in alcohol (tincture of iodine) is used as a disinfectant for wounds. Iodine vapour is harmful.

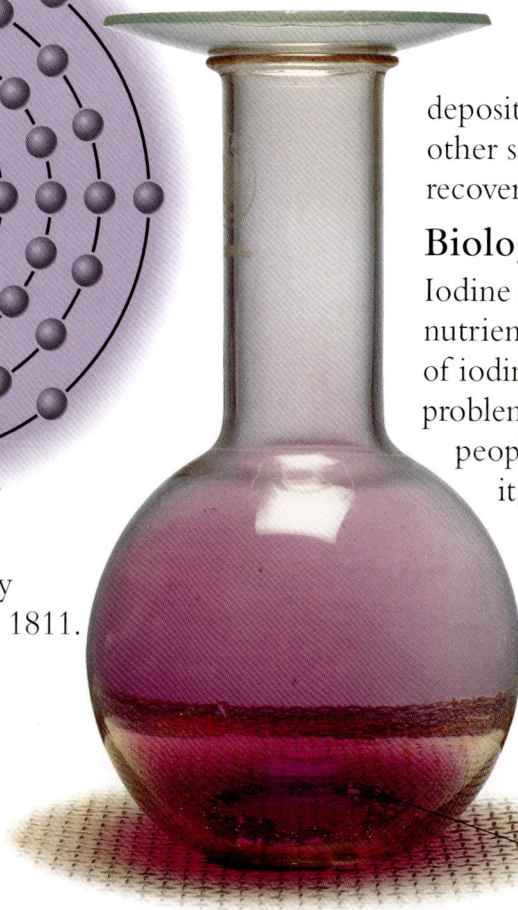

Violet iodine crystals sublimating into iodine vapour.

For more on iodine, see Volume 14: Chlorine, Fluorine, Bromine, and Iodine in the *Elements* set.

Iridium (Ir)

Element 77. One of the platinum metals among the transition metals in the Periodic Table. It is a precious (very rare), brittle, silvery-white metal. It is one of the densest materials known. It is obtained as a by-product of copper and nickel refining. Iridium is so unreactive that it cannot be dissolved even by concentrated acids. Only concentrated molten salts can dissolve it. That makes it the most corrosion-resistant metal known.

Discovery

It was discovered in 1803 by the English chemist Smithson Tennant.

Technology

Because it is so hard to obtain and to work, it is rarely used on its own. However, iridium is put into a platinum alloy. The alloy is harder and resists chemical attack better than platinum alone. It is in the alloyed form that platinum is usually made into jewellery. Until 1960 the standard metre was defined in terms of a bar made of a platinum–iridium alloy kept in Paris (it is now defined in terms of krypton).

Geology

It does not occur on its own as a native element, and it is very rare even in compounds. However, it appears in natural alloys with other noble metals such as platinum. It is normally obtained as a result of refining platinum.

Key facts...

Name: iridium
Symbol: Ir
Atomic number: 77
Atomic weight: 192.2
Position in Periodic Table: transition metal, group (9) (cobalt group); period 6. Precious metal
State at room temperature: solid
Colour: silvery-white
Density of solid: 22.5 g/cc
Melting point: 2,410°C
Boiling point: 4,527°C
Origin of name: from the Greek word *iris*, meaning rainbow, because its compounds have a wide variety of colours
Shell pattern of electrons: 2–8–18–32–15–2

Biology

Iridium does not occur in living things. Because it is so unreactive, it is harmless.

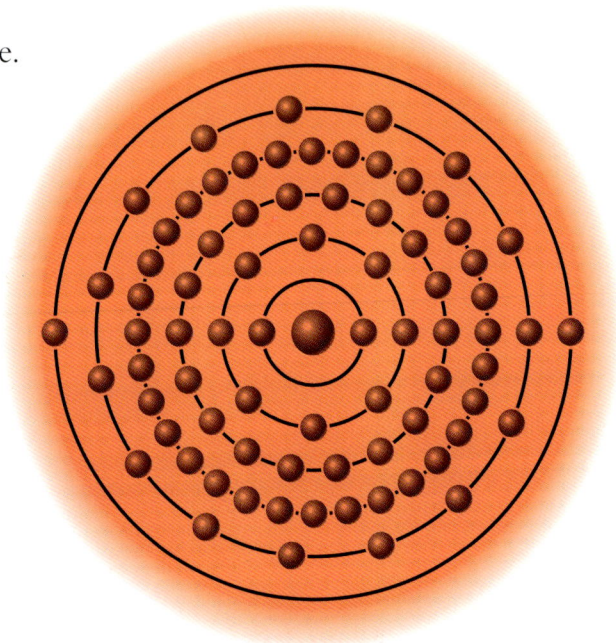

Iron (Fe)

Element 26. A common metal element belonging to the transition metals in the Periodic Table.

Iron makes up about a twentieth of the Earth's crust, being the second most abundant metal after aluminium. It is, however, far easier to separate it from its compounds than aluminium and has become the world's most useful metal. Iron is the most common magnetic element.

Iron is a steel-grey metal. It is quite reactive and readily corrodes to produce brown iron oxides, commonly known as rust.

Iron is also an important part of the human body. For example, it gives the red colour to blood.

Key facts...
Name: iron
Symbol: Fe
Atomic number: 26
Atomic weight: 55.84
Position in Periodic Table: transition metal, group (8) (iron group); period 4
State at room temperature: solid
Colour: steel-grey
Density of solid: 7.86 g/cc
Melting point: 1,538°C
Boiling point: 2,760°C
Origin of name: from the Anglo-Saxon word *iren*. The symbol Fe comes from the Latin word *ferrum*, meaning iron.
Shell pattern of electrons: 2–8–14–2

Refined iron contains about 4% carbon. That makes it quite brittle. When most of the carbon is removed, it becomes easier to work. It is then called steel.

Discovery

Known since ancient times. Its smelting led to the Iron Age.

▼ Small-scale production of iron by reacting iron oxide (iron ore) with powdered aluminium. A violent reaction takes place, reaching a temperature of over 2,000°C and producing molten iron and clouds of aluminium oxide smoke. This reaction, known as the thermit process, is used to weld railroad tracks together.

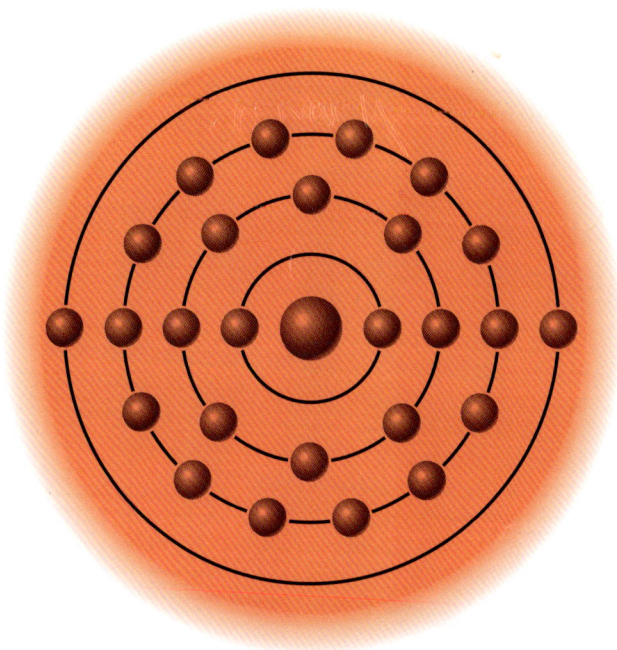

Technology

Iron is the most easily obtained, plentiful, and cheapest of all of the metals. Pure iron is rarely used because it corrodes so easily and is too soft. It is usually alloyed with carbon and other metals to make steel. Pig iron is an alloy containing about 3% carbon but also several non-metallic impurities. It is hard and brittle. It is the material produced by a blast furnace. Wrought iron contains less than 1% carbon, is not brittle and can be forged into shapes.

▲ Steel is purified iron with controlled amounts of other compounds added to give it useful properties.

▶ Gateway Arch, St. Louis, Missouri, is clad in stainless steel and shows how iron can be used to make large, strong structures in interesting shapes.

Geology

Iron is too reactive to occur as a native metal on the Earth's surface. It is found in the Earth's core and in stars. It is also found in compounds in the mantle and crust. The most common ore is haematite (iron (II) oxide, Fe_2O_3).

Biology

Iron is a vital element in all living things. It is particularly important for the oxygen-carrying blood cells as haemoglobin. Iron deficiency leads to anaemia, while an excess leads to kidney and liver damage.

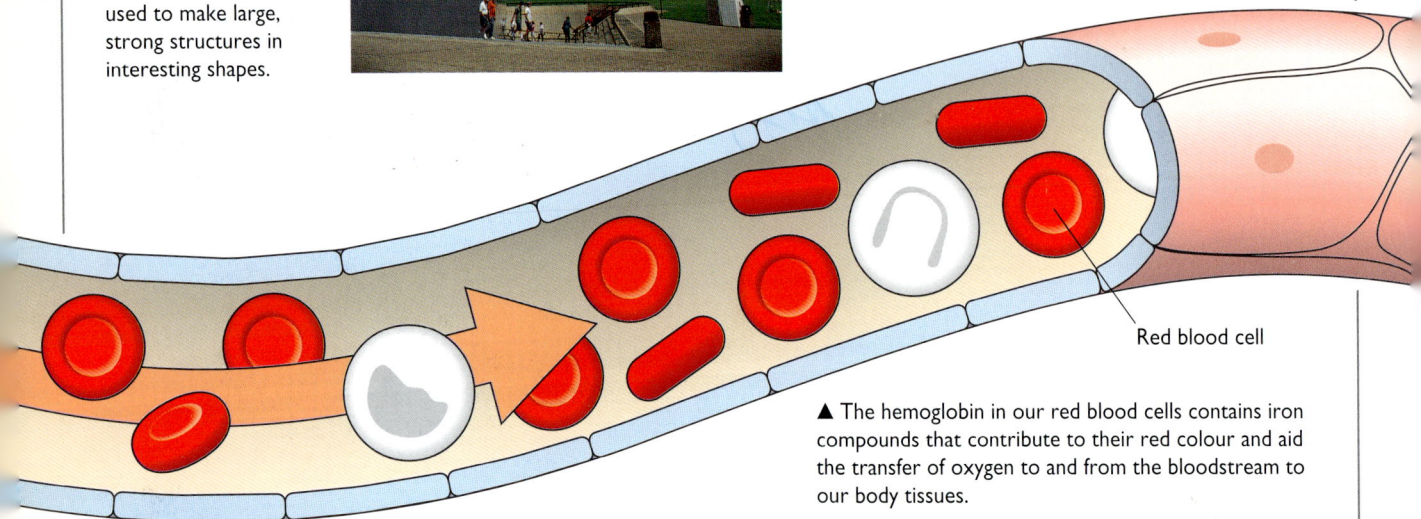

Red blood cell

▲ The hemoglobin in our red blood cells contains iron compounds that contribute to their red colour and aid the transfer of oxygen to and from the bloodstream to our body tissues.

For more on iron, see Volume 4: Iron, Chromium, and Manganese in the *Elements* set.

Krypton (Kr)

Element 36. One of the noble gases in group 8 in the Periodic Table. It is an inert gas and forms very few compounds.

Krypton is heavier than air, colourless, odourless and tasteless. It produces brilliant green and orange lines in a spectroscope (an instrument for finding the natural colours emitted from an element). The fundamental unit of length, the metre, is defined as 1m = 1,650,763.73 wavelengths of the orange–red line of krypton.

When a current of electricity is passed through a glass tube containing krypton at low pressure, it gives out a bluish-white light.

Discovery

Krypton was discovered in 1898 by the British chemists Sir William Ramsay and Morris W. Travers in the liquid that remained after liquid air had nearly boiled away.

Technology

Krypton can be used on its own or with argon and neon as the gas in incandescent (ordinary) bulbs. Electric-discharge tubes filled with krypton are used to light airfields because the red light they give out can be seen from far away and also penetrates fog and haze better than ordinary light. Krypton is used in some types of fluorescent lamps and for flash lamps used in high-speed photography. However, it is not widely used because of its high cost of production.

Key facts...

Name: krypton
Symbol: Kr
Atomic number: 36
Atomic weight: 83.80
Position in Periodic Table: group 8 (18) (noble gases); period 4
State at room temperature: gas
Colour: colourless
Density of gas ay 20°C: 3.48 g/cc
Melting point: –157°C
Boiling point: –152°C
Origin of name: from the Greek word *kryptos*, meaning hidden
Shell pattern of electrons: 2–8–18–8

Geology

Krypton is found in the air in about one part per million. It is also found in the atmosphere of Mars.

Biology

Krypton is not found in living things, but since it is inert, it is not harmful.

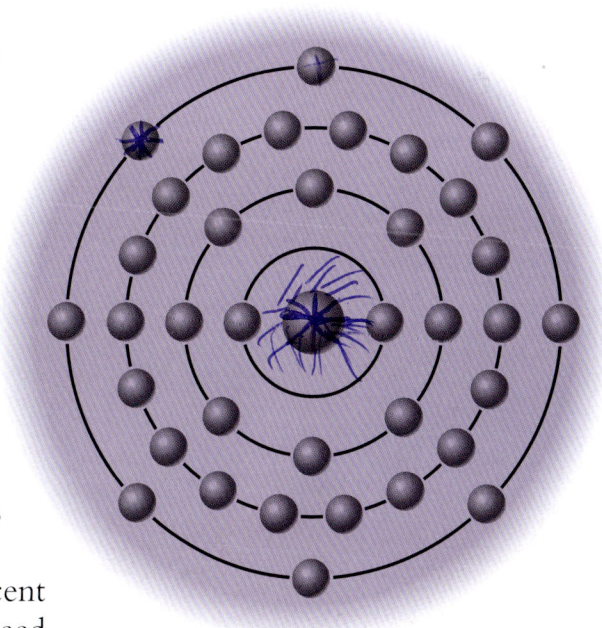

For more on krypton, see Volume 1: Hydrogen and the Noble Gases in the *Elements* set.

Lanthanum (La)

Element 57. The first member of the rare-earth metals (lanthanide series) in the Periodic Table.

Lanthanum is a soft, silvery-white metal that is easy to bend (ductile) and form into new shapes (malleable). The metal can be cut with a knife.

Lanthanum is one of the more reactive rare earths and oxidises rapidly in air. Although it corrodes only slowly in cold water, it corrodes very quickly in hot water. Lanthanum reacts directly with elemental carbon, nitrogen, boron, selenium, silicon, phosphorus, sulphur and with halogens.

Discovery

It was discovered in Sweden in 1839 by Carl Gustaf Mosander. The name lanthanum comes from the Greek word *lanthanein*, meaning to escape notice. Lanthanum is quite common, being 28th in abundance of the elements in the Earth's crust.

Technology

Lanthanum oxide goes into high-quality glass lenses because it improves the alkali resistance of glass. It is also used in high-intensity lighting, such as for movie projectors and studio lighting.

Geology

Not found as a native metal, but as the phosphate minerals apatite, xenotime, monazite, and bastnasite, as well as in calcite and fluorspar.

Biology

Lanthanum is not found in living things.

Key facts...

Name: Lanthanum
Symbol: La
Atomic number: 57
Atomic weight: 138.9
Position in Periodic Table: inner transition metal; period 6 (lanthanide series)
State at room temperature: solid
Colour: silvery-white
Density of solid: 6.17 g/cc
Melting point: 920°C
Boiling point: 3,454°C
Origin of name: from the Greek word *lanthanein*, meaning to be concealed, because it was particularly difficult to separate from its compounds
Shell pattern of electrons: 2–8–18–18–9–2

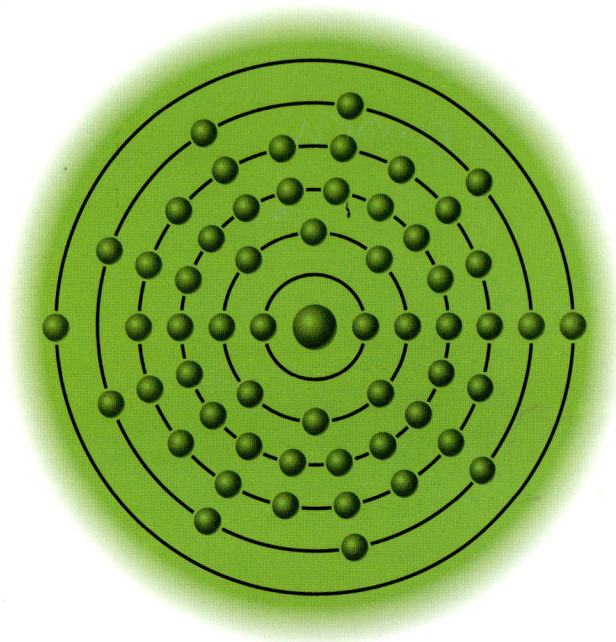

Lawrencium (Lr)

Element 103. An artificial and radioactive element among the transition metals in the Periodic Table.

Discovery

It was produced in 1961 at Berkeley, California, by Albert Ghiorso, T. Sikkeland, A. E. Larsh, and R.M. Latimer by bombarding californium with boron ions accelerated in a heavy-ion linear accelerator. This produced short-lived isotopes of lawrencium.

Technology

Very little lawrencium (about 2 micrograms) has been produced, and so far no one has found any uses for it.

Geology

Lawrencium is not found naturally in the environment.

Biology

Lawrencium does not occur in living things; but because it is radioactive, it could be harmful if produced in substantial quantities.

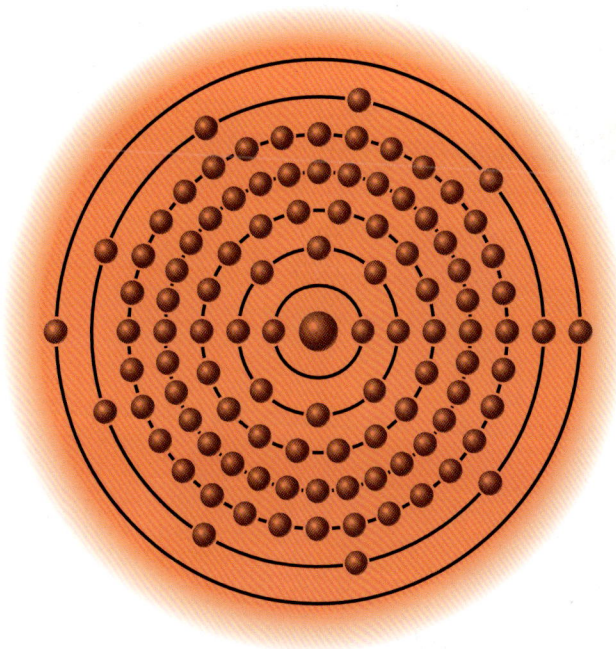

Lead (Pb)

Element 82. A soft, bluish–white metal in group 4 (the carbon group) in the Periodic Table.

Lead is very dense, soft and easily shaped. However, it is a relatively poor conductor of electricity. When lead is exposed to the air, it quickly develops a coating that makes it dull brown. This coating (similar in effect to the coating that develops on copper) then helps prevent further reaction, and corrosion happens very slowly.

It is also used in low-melting-point alloys, such as solder, and in pewter. Lead will absorb sound and radiation, so it is used for soundproofing and as a protection against radiation. It was also once used as an antiknock ingredient in petrol, but lead is poisonous and so has been taken out of petrol and is no longer used in water pipes.

Lead is mainly found in the mineral lead sulphide (also called galena).

Key facts...
Name: lead
Symbol: Pb
Atomic number: 82
Atomic weight: 207.2
Position in Periodic Table: group 4 (14) (carbon group); period 6
State at room temperature: solid
Colour: bluish-white
Density of solid: 11.3 g/cc
Melting point: 327°C
Boiling point: 1,744°C
Origin of name: from the Anglo-Saxon word *lead*; the symbol is from the Latin, *plumbum*, meaning liquid silver
Shell pattern of electrons: 2–8–18–32–18–4

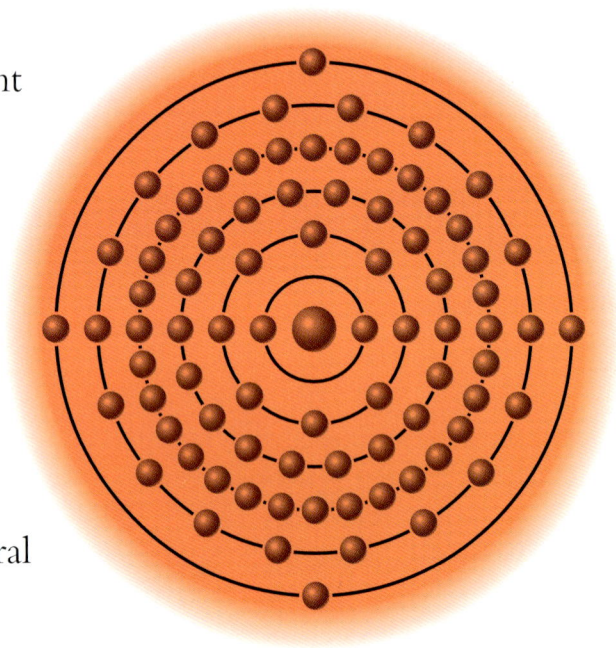

◀ Lead metal showing its cubic structure.

Discovery

Known since ancient times.

Technology

The low reactivity of lead means it does well as a container for corrosive materials such as acids, as a roofing material and to protect underground wires. In the past it was also used for water pipes and in paints, but that has largely stopped owing to possible health hazards. Lead also goes into plates for storage batteries, such as those in cars. Lead is an additive in lead glass, from which cut and crystal glassware are made. It is also an additive in special lenses.

Geology

Native lead is sometimes found as crystals in hydrothermal veins close to old volcanic magma chambers. It more frequently appears as sulphide and carbonate compounds. Among the most common compounds are galena (lead sulphide, PbS) and cerussite (lead carbonate, $PbCO_3$). Galena is the main mineral from which lead is refined.

Biology

Lead does not naturally occur in living things. However, when lead gets into the body, it affects the central nervous system and can cause brain damage. Lead does not easily leave the body and builds up over the years. That is why small doses, such as are found in air polluted by leaded gas emissions, can be dangerous, especially for children.

▲ Lead is used as a shield against radiation. This laboratory chamber is used for handling radioactive materials and so has lead glass and solid lead walls.

Molten lead

▶ If an orange form of lead (II) oxide (called litharge) is heated on a carbon block, it first turns yellow (a form of lead (II) oxide called missicot) before being reduced to molten lead. Colourless carbon monoxide gas is given off during the reaction.

For more on lead, see Volume 10: Lead and Tin in the *Elements* set.

Lithium (Li)

Element 3. A member of the alkali metals, group 1 in the Periodic Table.

Lithium is a soft, silvery-white, shiny metal that has only half the density of water. It is very reactive and rapidly tarnishes in air. Lithium metal has the highest specific heat of any solid element. Lithium salts colour flames bright red.

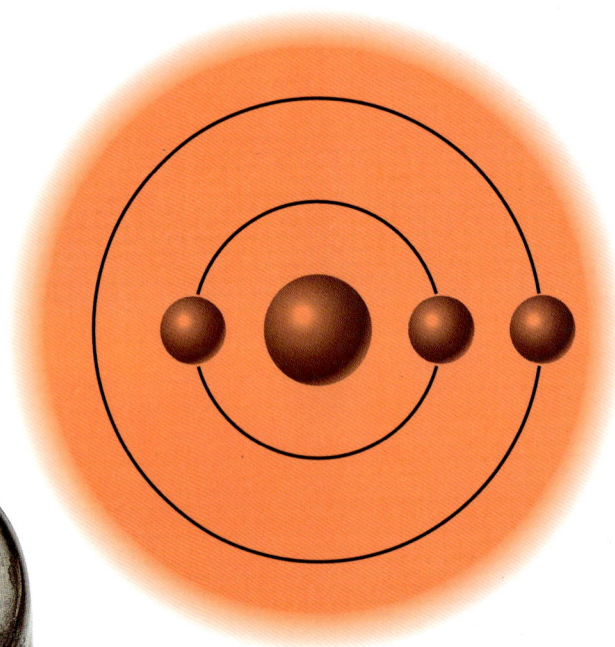

Discovery

Lithium was discovered in Stockholm, Sweden in 1817 by Johan August Arfwedson.

Technology

Lithium is alloyed with aluminium, lead, and other soft metals to make them harder and so more useful in, for example, aircraft manufacture. Lithium also goes into some batteries as well as high-strength glass. Lithium is added to oils to make a high-temperature lubricant. Lithium hydroxide can absorb carbon dioxide in space vehicles.

A lithium battery

Geology

Because it is highly reactive, lithium does not occur as a native element. It is found in most igneous rocks as a minor component.

Lithium is obtained from the ore spodumene, $LiAl(SiO_3)_2$ and is also extracted from brine in salt lakes.

Biology

Not a natural part of living matter, but affects moods in humans and is used as a mental-health medicine.

Lutetium (Lu)

Element 71. It is a rare-earth element and belongs to the transition metals in the Periodic Table. It is a silvery-white metal that reacts slowly and so is quite stable in air.

Discovery

Lutetium was discovered separately in France in 1907 by Georges Urbain and in Austria by Carl Auer von Welsbach. Georges Urbain named the element lutetium, which was based on the word *Lutetia*, the Latin name for Paris. Lutetium was spelled 'lutecium' until 1949.

Technology

A natural radioactive isotope of lutetium (with a half-life of 30 billion years) is used to date meteorites in comparison with the age of the Earth. Lutetium can help break up (crack) crude oil and can make some alloys. However, it is very expensive to prepare.

Geology

Lutetium is never found as a native metal, but is found in the minerals monazite (a phosphate mineral) and bastnasite (a carbonate mineral), as well as in all minerals that contain yttrium.

Biology

Lutetium is not found in living things, but is not regarded as especially harmful.

Key facts...

Name: lutetium
Symbol: Lu
Atomic number: 71
Atomic weight: 174.96
Position in Periodic Table: transition metal, group (3) (scandium group); period 6
State at room temperature: solid
Colour: silvery-white
Density of solid: 9.84 g/cc
Melting point: 1,652°C
Boiling point: 3,315°C
Origin of the name: from the Latin *Lutetia*, meaning Paris
Shell pattern of electrons: 2–8–18–32–9–2

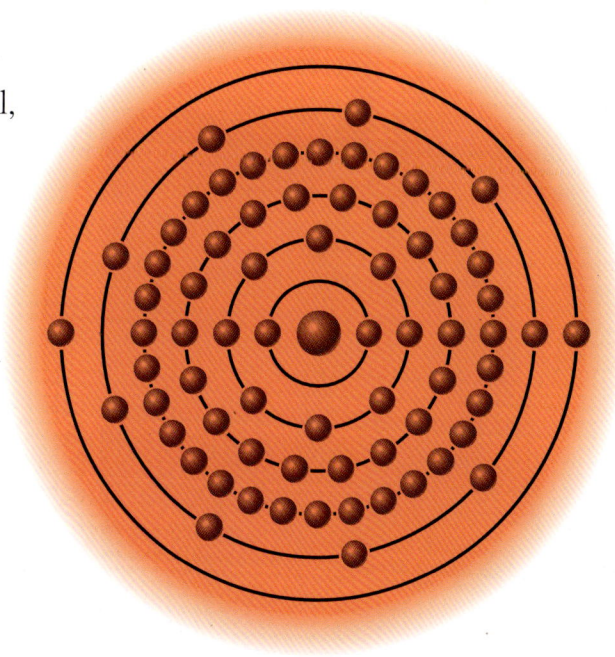

Magnesium (Mg)

Element 12. A silvery-white, soft and reactive member of the alkaline earth metals, group 2 in the Periodic Table. It is the eighth most common element in the Earth's crust.

Magnesium is very reactive, never found as a native element and quickly tarnishes in air. The oxide coating then protects it from further reactions with air and water (making it appear unreactive) unless the surface is cleaned off. Magnesium burns with an intense white flame.

Discovery

Magnesium was first identified as an element by Joseph Black in 1755 but not isolated until 1808 by Sir Humphry Davy in England. That was done by electrolysis of magnesium oxide (MgO).

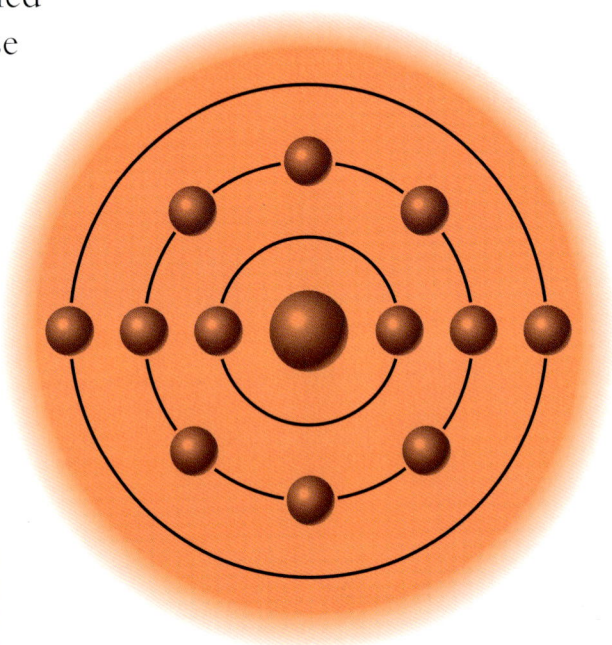

Technology

It is the lightest metal that is regularly used in construction (lighter than aluminium) and is widely used in aircraft and for space vehicles. It is alloyed with aluminium, zinc and manganese to improve its strength.

◀ A cleaned strip of magnesium ribbon burns in air with an intense white light. The result is white magnesium oxide.

Geology

Magnesium is common in sea water and in evaporite deposits (dried ancient lake beds). Dolomite, a form of limestone, is $MgCa(CO_3)_2$.

Biology

Magnesium is also important in living things. In plants the green pigment chlorophyll is a compound of magnesium. Magnesium is needed in animals to make some enzymes work. People need about 0.3g of magnesium each day.

Compounds of magnesium include those used in medicine, such as Epsom salts (magnesium sulphate, $MgSO_4$) and milk of magnesia (magnesium carbonate, $MgCO_2$).

Epsom salts were named after Epsom, south of London, England, where the magnesium mineral was first discovered in well water. Magnesium salts make the water taste bitter.

Magnesium salts are not harmful to health.

▲▼ A piece of dolomite. This hard rock, which contains magnesium carbonate, produces sharp peaks and dramatic scenery that is characteristic of the Dolomites, a mountain range in the southern Alps of northeastern Italy.

For more on magnesium, see Volume 3: Calcium and Magnesium in the *Elements* set.

Manganese (Mn)

Element 25. A silvery-white, hard, brittle metal belonging to the transition metals in the Periodic Table. Manganese is very reactive in air.

Discovery

It was discovered in 1774 by the Swedish chemist Carl Wilhelm Scheele using the mineral pyrolusite (manganese dioxide, MnO_2) heated with charcoal (carbon), which smelted the ore and released the metal.

Technology

The main use of manganese is as an alloy to make steel easier to work. Manganese steel is also hard wearing and corrosion resistant. It is also used with steel, aluminium, antimony and copper to make magnets. All aluminium and magnesium alloys have manganese in them to improve their wearability and corrosion resistance.

Manganese can take away any colour staining in glass that has been tinted by iron impurities.

Potassium permanganate ($KMnO_4$) is a disinfectant.

Geology

Manganese is not found as the free metal in nature. It lends the colour purple to the mineral amethyst and is common in a range of other minerals, some of which appear abundantly as nodules on the deep ocean floors.

Biology

Manganese compounds are essential to the enzymes that are vital to all living things. A lack of manganese causes bone deformities and infertility.

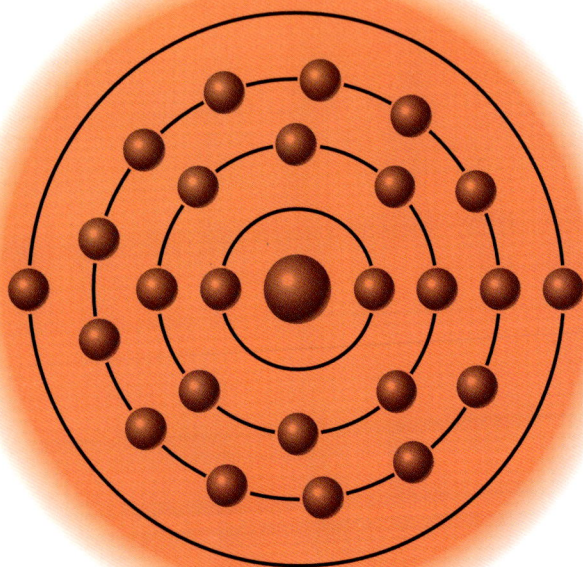

For more on manganese, see Volume 4: Iron, Chromium, and Manganese in the *Elements* set.

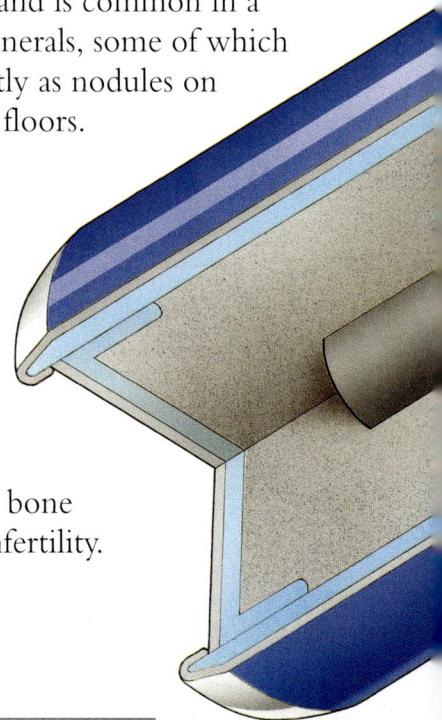

Meitnerium (Mt)

Element 109. Also formerly called unnilennium (Une). It is an artificially produced radioactive element belonging to the transition metals in the Periodic Table. It is a transuranium element. Only a single nucleus of the element has so far been identified.

Discovery

It was discovered in 1982 at the Institute for Heavy Ion Research in Germany, when bismuth 209 was bombarded with iron 58 ions.

Technology

It has no uses.

Key facts...

Name: Meitnerium
Symbol: Mt
Atomic number: 109
Atomic weight: 266
Position in Periodic Table: transition metal, group (9) (cobalt group); period 7
State at room temperature: solid
Colour: unknown
Density: n/a
Melting point: n/a
Boiling point: n/a
Origin of name: named after Lise Meitner, the Austrian physicist
Shell pattern of electrons: 2–8–18–32–32–15–2

Geology

Because it is an artificial element, it is not found in the environment.

Biology

It is not found in living things.

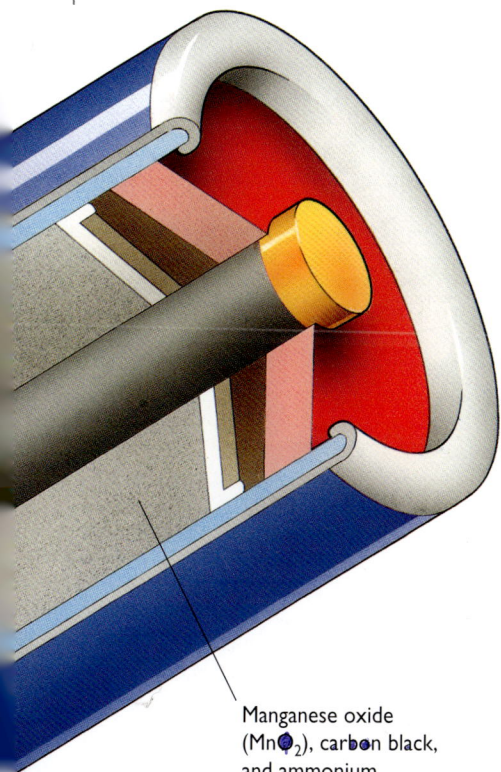

Manganese oxide (MnO_2), carbon black, and ammonium chloride (NH_4Cl)

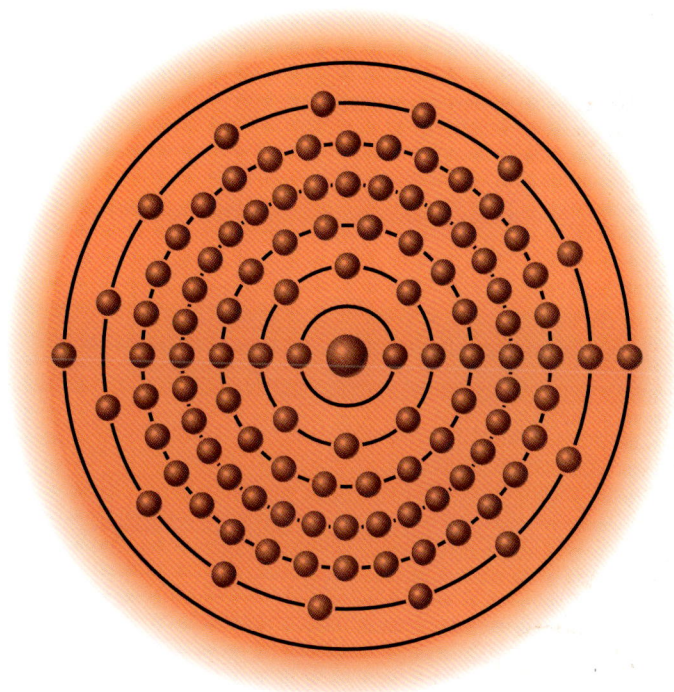

Mendelevium (Md)

Element 101. An artificial and radioactive chemical element in the actinide series in the Periodic Table.

Discovery

It was discovered by Albert Ghiorso, Bernard G. Harvey, Gregory R. Choppin, Stanley G. Thompson, and Glenn T. Seaborg at the University of California, Berkeley, in 1955 when helium ions were bombarded at a tiny amount of einsteinium-253. Mendelevium was the first element to be made one atom at a time. Mendelevium-258 (the most stable isotope) has a half-life of about 54 days. It was the ninth transuranium element of the actinide series to be discovered.

Technology

Because it has only been produced in such small quantities, so far it has no uses.

Geology

Because it is artificial, it is not found in the environment.

Biology

It is not found in living things; but if it were ever produced in substantial quantities, it could be harmful because it is radioactive.

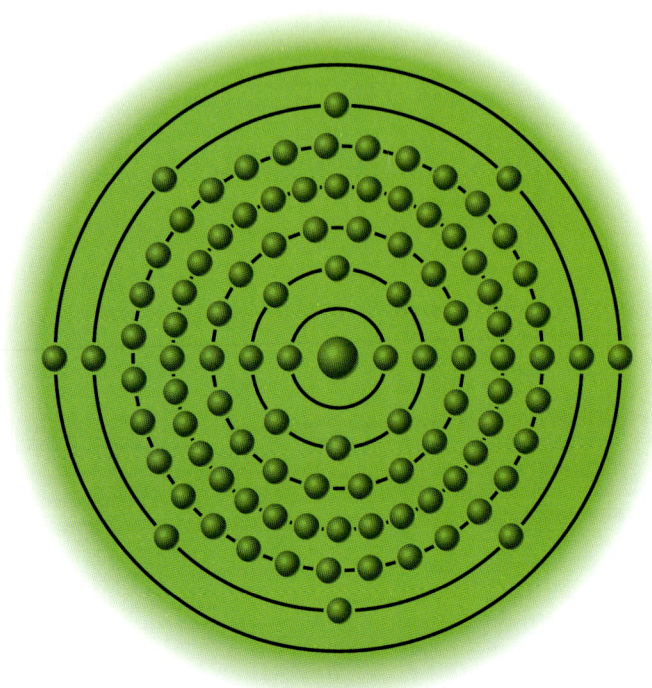

Mercury (Hg)

Element 80. Mercury, which is also called quicksilver, is a silvery-coloured liquid metal belonging to the transition metals in the Periodic Table. It is the heaviest known liquid element.

Mercury is the only metal element that is liquid at room temperature. It has very good electrical conductivity but is a poor conductor of heat.

Discovery

It has been known since ancient times.

Technology

Since it is liquid at room temperature and does not cling to glass, it is used in thermometers. Because of its high density it is used in Fortin-type barometers. Since it conducts electricity, it is also goes into special sealed switches.

Key facts...

Name: mercury
Symbol: Hg
Atomic number: 80
Atomic weight: 200.59 (2)
Position in Periodic Table: transition metal, group (12), (zinc group); period 6
State at room temperature: liquid
Colour: silvery
Density of liquid: 13.6 g/cc
Melting point: –39°C
Boiling point: 357°C
Origin of name: named after the planet Mercury. The symbol Hg is from the Latin word *hydrargyrum*, meaning liquid silver
Shell pattern of electrons: 2–8–18–32–18–2

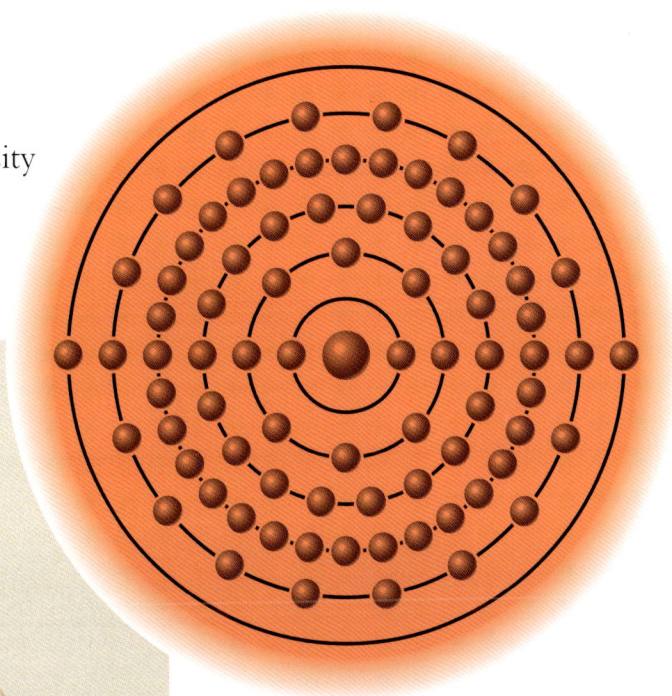

◄ When a solution of yellow potassium chromate is dropped into a colourless solution of mercuric nitrate, an orange precipitate of mercuric chromate forms.

When electricity is passed through mercury vapour, it gives off a bluish glow, so it is used in street lighting and in fluorescent lamps. Mercury is alloyed with many metals to form amalgams. Amalgams are used in dental fillings.

Geology

It is occasionally found as a native liquid metal, but much more commonly as the red mineral cinnabar (mercury sulphide, HgS). Mercury is a rare element.

Biology

Mercury vapour is poisonous. It can be absorbed by breathing, through contact with the skin and by absorption in the digestive system. It is not easily removed from the system and builds up in the body. It is not safe to be in a room with free liquid mercury.

All mercury compounds are extremely toxic. Yet mercury is used to remove gold from its ores, which releases vapours that are toxic. Many gold miners in developing countries suffer from their effects.

Mercury affects the central nervous system. It used to be used in hat making, and its effect on hatters gave rise to the term 'mad as a hatter'. Mercury poisoning can also come about from the improper disposal of mercury wastes from factories. One example, in the sea around Japan, led to many deaths.

Mercurous chloride Hg_2Cl_2 (as calomel) has been used as a medicine.

▲ Mercury's strong surface tension keeps the liquid formed as small globules.

For more on mercury, see 6: Zinc, Cadmium, and Mercury in the *Elements* set.

Molybdenum (Mo)

Element 42. A rare, silvery-grey and hard metal belonging to the transition metals in the Periodic Table. It was often confused with graphite and lead ore.

Discovery

Carl William Scheele discovered it in 1778 in a sample of the ore now known as molybdenite. It was thought to be an ore of lead at that time.

Technology

Molybdenum makes an alloy that strengthens and increases the melting point of steel. It also improves corrosion resistance. It goes into electrodes in electrically heated glass furnaces. It has an important role as a catalyst in petroleum refining and is a good fuel additive that can lubricate the upper cylinder head of a combustion engine and so increase fuel efficiency. It can also be made into a filament for heating wires.

Geology

Molybdenum is not found as a native element. The most important ore is molybdenite (molybdenum sulphide, MoS_2).

Key facts...

Name: molybdenum
Symbol: Mo
Atomic number: 42
Atomic weight: 95.94
Position in Periodic Table: transition metal, group (6) (chromium group); period 5
State at room temperature: solid
Colour: silvery-grey
Density of solid: 10.2 g/cc
Melting point: 2,610°C
Boiling point: 5,560°C
Origin of name: from the Greek word *molybdos* for lead, because it looks like lead
Shell pattern of electrons: 2–8–18–13–1

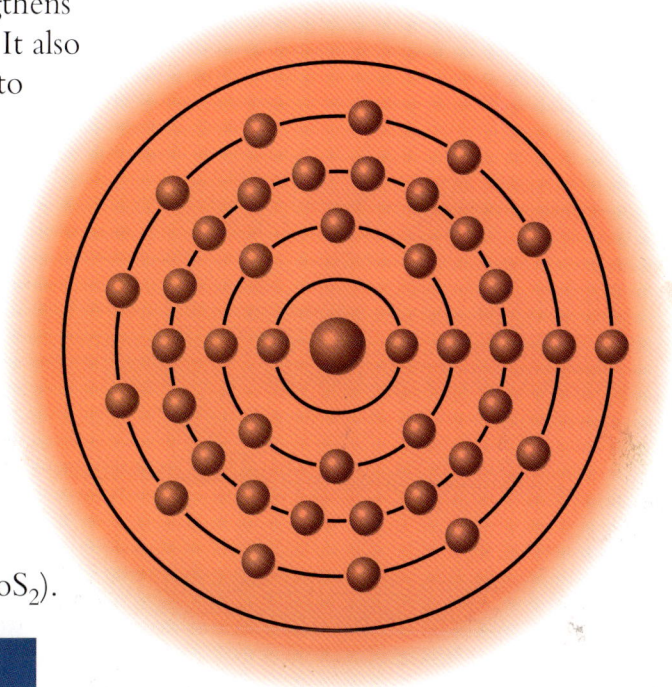

▲ The Climax Mine, high in the Colourado Rockies, is the largest source of molybdenite – the principal ore of molybdenum.

Molybdenum also appears in other ores and is often recovered as a by-product of non-ferrous copper refining.

Biology

Molybdenum is an essential trace element in all living things. A lack of it can make a soil infertile, while its presence helps bacteria fix nitrogen in the soil.

Neodymium (Nd)

Element 60. A silvery-white rare-earth metal (lanthanide) in the Periodic Table. It quickly reacts in air to form a brittle oxide coating that flakes and exposes more metal to the air. Thus, unless it is sealed in plastic or kept under oil, it quickly disintegrates.

Discovery

Discovered in Austria in 1885 by Carl F. Auer von Welsbach using a sample of the mineral samarskite. He found two elements: neodymium and praseodymium.

Technology

Neodymium is used in alloys (especially misch metal, which contains 15% neodymium), for cigarette lighter flints, and in electronics. It colours glass a pure violet and in smaller amounts removes the green colouring caused by iron impurities in glass. Neodymium glass can replace a ruby inside a laser. It makes protective glass for welding goggles and shields because it absorbs harmful radiation from the welding process. Because it absorbs some kinds of light very strongly, in astronomy it helps calibrate spectrometers that explore the chemical make-up of the universe. Neodymium alloyed with iron also makes a powerful permanent magnet.

Geology

Neodymium is too reactive to be found as a native element. It appears mainly in the minerals xenotime, monazite and bastnasite.

Biology

Neodymium is not found in living things.

Key facts...
Name: neodymium
Symbol: Nd
Atomic number: 60
Atomic weight: 144.2
Position in Periodic Table: inner transition metal; period 6 (lanthanide series)
State at room temperature: solid
Colour: silvery-white
Density of solid: 7.00 g/cc
Melting point: 1,021°C
Boiling point: 3,168°C
Origin of name: from the Greek words *neos* and *didymos*, meaning new twin
Shell pattern of electrons: 2–8–18–22–8–2

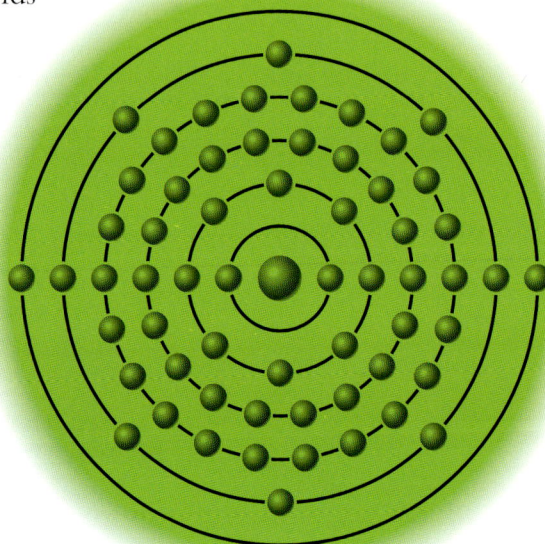

Neon (Ne)

Element 10. A colourless, odourless and tasteless inert gas from group 8, the noble gases, in the Periodic Table.

Neon forms no stable compounds because it is unreactive.

Discovery

Neon was discovered in 1898 by the British chemists Sir William Ramsay and Morris W. Travers.

Technology

Neon glows reddish–orange in a vacuum tube when an electric current is passed through it. The strength of the glow is much greater than for any other gas. That is why its main use is in neon signs. Neon also makes a very effective refrigerating fluid in experiments and a gas laser.

Key facts...

Name: neon
Symbol: Ne
Atomic number: 10
Atomic weight: 20.18
Position in Periodic Table: group 8 (18) (noble gases); period 2
State at room temperature: gas
Colour: colourless
Density of gas at 20°C: 1.17 g/l
Melting point: –248.59°C
Boiling point: –246.08°C
Origin of name: from the Greek word *neon*, meaning new
Shell pattern of electrons: 2–8

Geology

Neon is found in tiny quantities in the atmosphere (0.0018% by volume in dry air). Most neon is recovered by liquefying air and then allowing the neon to boil off for collection.

Biology

Neon is not present in living things.

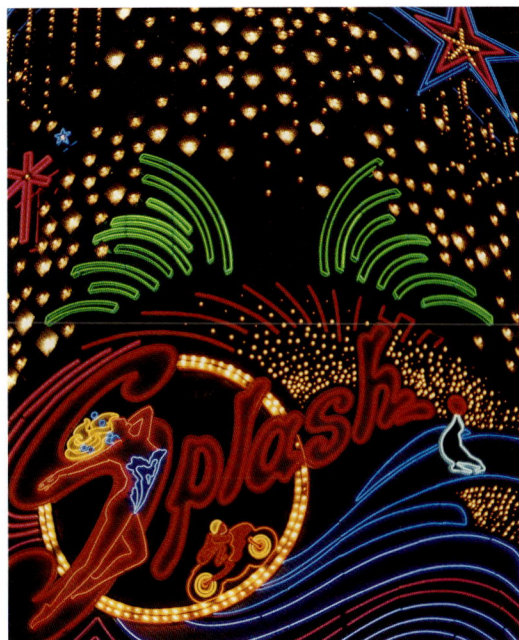

▲ All lights in discharge tubes are generally called 'neon'; however, neon only emits a reddish-orange glow. Each of the rare gases produces a different 'neon' colour. For example, helium produces a yellow 'neon' light when an electric current flows through it.

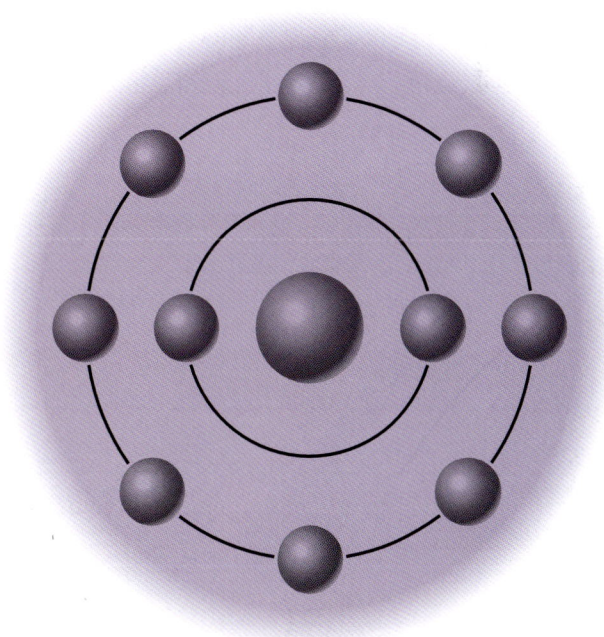

For more on neon, see Volume 1: Hydrogen and the Noble Gases in the *Elements* set.

Neptunium (Np)

Element 93. It is a silver-coloured radioactive rare-earth metal element in the actinide series in the Periodic Table. It is a reactive element with properties similar to uranium.

In 1940 it became the first transuranium element to be artificially produced as a by-product in nuclear reactors.

Key facts...
Name: neptunium
Symbol: Np
Atomic number: 93
Atomic weight: 237
Position in Periodic Table: inner transition metal; period 7 (actinide series)
State at room temperature: solid
Colour: silvery
Density of solid: 20.45 g/cc
Melting point: 640°C
Boiling point: 4,000°C
Origin of name: named after the planet Neptune
Shell pattern of electrons: 2–8–18–32–22–9–2

Discovery

Discovered by Edwin M. McMillan and P. H. Abelson in California in 1940 when they bombarded uranium with neutrons. At that time only elements as far as uranium in the Periodic Table had been discovered. That made it the first transuranium element (that is, an element after uranium) ever produced.

Technology

Used in neutron-detecting equipment.

Geology

Very small amounts of neptunium are found in association with uranium ores. But most neptunium is recovered from spent fuel rods from nuclear reactors.

Biology

Neptunium is not found in living things.

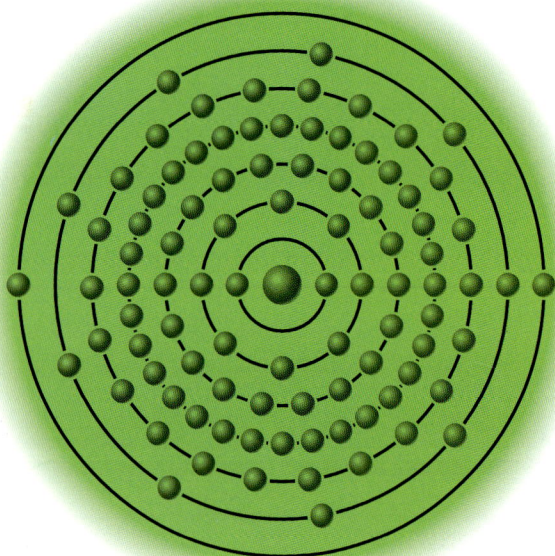

Nickel (Ni)

Element 28. A silvery, hard magnetic transition metal element in the Periodic Table that is easily bent and made into new shapes. Nickel has some magnetic properties. It is a fair conductor of heat and electricity.

It is similar to iron in many of its properties, but it reacts more slowly and resists corrosion.

Discovery

It was discovered in 1751 by a Swedish chemist, Baron Axel Fredrik Cronstedt. He was trying to extract copper from the ore niccolite but instead got a shiny metal (nickel) that, as a result of his surprise, he then called false copper, or copper demon (*kupfernickel*).

Technology

It is one of the main metals used in 'silver' coins. The 5-cent US coin (the nickel) contains 25% nickel. However, the jeweller's 'nickel silver' contains no silver at all. Nickel is widely used in alloys; an alloy of nickel and iron makes stainless steel. It also makes a protective coating on steel. Nickel steel is made into armour plating. A copper–nickel alloy is very corrosion resistant and is used in tubing for desalination plants. Finely divided nickel can be a catalyst and also goes into batteries.

Nickel ore.

Geology

Nickel is found in most meteorites. Iron meteorites can contain up to one fifth nickel.

Biology

Nickel is an essential trace element for many living things.

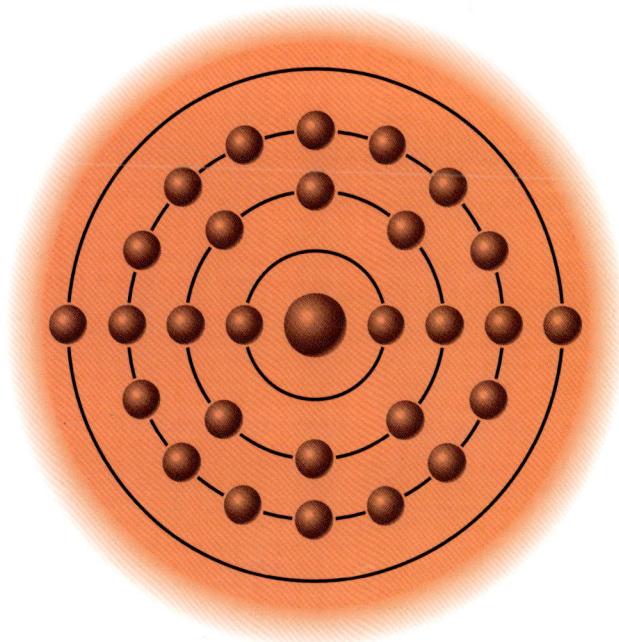

Niobium (Nb)

Element 41. A soft, shiny, white and easily shaped (ductile) metal belonging to the transition metals in the Periodic Table.

It looks like steel with a bluish tinge when kept in air, but looks more like platinum when polished. It is used in alloys, in particular in some stainless steels to give extra strength.

Discovery

It was first discovered in 1801 by the English chemist Charles Hatchett, who isolated it from the ore columbite, which had been sent to England in the 1750s by John Winthrop the Younger, the first governor of Connecticut.

Heinrich Rose named the element niobium, which has since been used in place of the original name 'columbium'. It took until 1864 for pure niobium metal to be isolated.

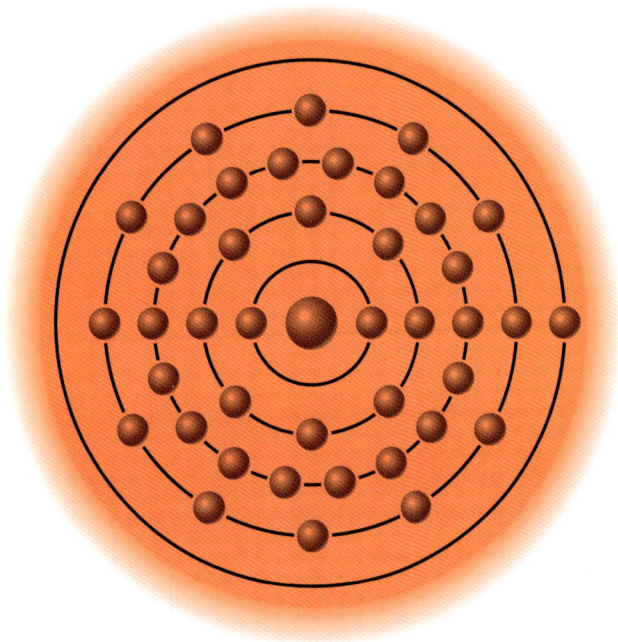

Technology

Niobium is alloyed with iron as part of stainless steel. The alloying adds strength, and niobium alloys are used in pipelines. Niobium alloys are used as a source of arc welding rods for welding stainless steel. It also alloys with non-ferrous metals. Niobium is also used for some body-art decoration such as metal rings.

Geology

Because niobium is a reactive element, it is not found in native form. It often occurs in ores with tantalum, which is chemically similar. Niobite is a complex ore containing iron, manganese, tantalum and niobium.

Biology

Niobium is not found in living things. Its compounds are toxic.

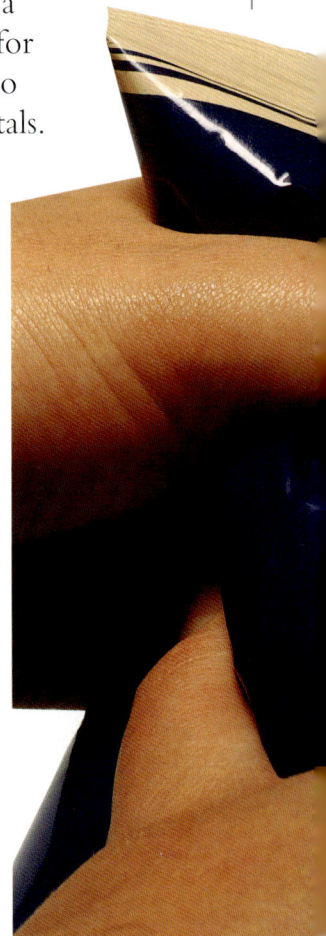

Nitrogen (N)

Element 7. An almost inert (unreactive) gas at ordinary temperature and pressure. It is a colourless, odourless and tasteless non-metallic element in group 5 (the nitrogen group) in the Periodic Table. Nitrogen is the sixth most common element in the universe. It is the most common element in the atmosphere, making up 78% of the air and it is also found in all living matter.

Nitrogen is made by liquefying air.

When nitrogen is heated, it combines with magnesium, lithium, and calcium. Under pressure it combines with hydrogen to form ammonia. This is called the Haber process. When mixed with

Key facts...

Name: nitrogen
Symbol: N
Atomic number: 7
Atomic weight: 14.01
Position in Periodic Table: group 5 (15) (nitrogen group); period 2
State at room temperature: gas
Colour: colourless
Density of gas at 20°C: 1.17 g/l
Melting point: −209.86°C
Boiling point: −196°C
Origin of name: the French chemist Antoine Lavoisier named it *azote* because no living thing could survive in it (from the Greek word meaning life). This term is still used in French. The name nitrogen was coined in 1790 after a common mineral then known as nitre (potassium nitrate) from *niter* and *-gen*, meaning nitre-forming.
Shell pattern of electrons: 2–5

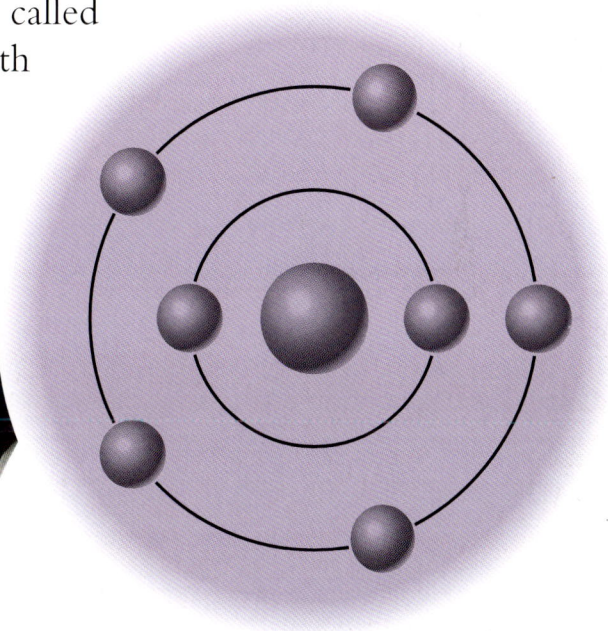

◀ The puffed-up packaging that is used for some foods is not just to make the food appear to occupy more volume than it really does. The bag contains inert nitrogen, used to prevent the food from spoiling and, in the case of delicate foods like crisps, to help prevent the packaging from being crushed and the crisps breaking.

oxygen and in the presence of ans electric spark such as a flash of lightning or from a spark plug in a car engine, it forms nitric oxide (NO) and then the dioxide (NO_2). Oxides of nitrogen are poisonous. Nitrogen dioxide is one of the main pollutants of the atmosphere and a producer of ground-level ozone.

Discovery

Nitrogen was discovered by Daniel Rutherford in Scotland in 1772, who originally called it noxious air because it is the main part of the air but, unlike oxygen, does not support life.

Technology

Nitrogen is mainly used in the form of ammonia for fertilisers. It also goes into explosives such as nitroglycerin.

It is widely used to keep air away from food during food preparation. Freeze–drying is done in an atmosphere of nitrogen. Liquid nitrogen can expel oil from underground oilfields or also play a safety role by filling tanks that normally contain explosive liquids.

Geology

Few minerals contain nitrogen. The main nitrate mineral is saltpetre (sodium nitrate, $NaNO_3$), a soluble mineral.

Biology

Nitrogen forms part of one of the world's most important natural cycles, the nitrogen cycle. It is an essential part of many molecules that are made from amino acids. Animals get nitrogen for their tissues by eating vegetable or animal proteins. Nitrogen is fixed from the atmosphere by

bacteria living on the roots of some plants such as peas, usually called legumes. Nitrogen is added to fields by farmers wanting to get increased yields. Some nitrogen seeps from the fields into rivers and can cause pollution. Some nitrogen compounds such as cyanide are highly poisonous. Nitrogen oxides from vehicle combustion help produce acid rain and can be an irritant.

Nitrogen group elements

Another term for the group 5 elements in the Periodic Table, which include nitrogen (N), phosphorus (P), arsenic (As), antimony (Sb) and bismuth (Bi).

▼ Nitric oxide is a colourless gas. When mixed with air, it reacts with oxygen to produce brown nitrogen dioxide.

For more on nitrogen, see Volume 11: Nitrogen and Phosphorus in the *Elements* set.

Nobelium (No)

Element 102. An artificial and radioactive metal element in the actinide series in the Periodic Table. The properties of this element are unknown because so little has been isolated; but because it is an actinide, it is expected that its properties should be similar to other rare earths.

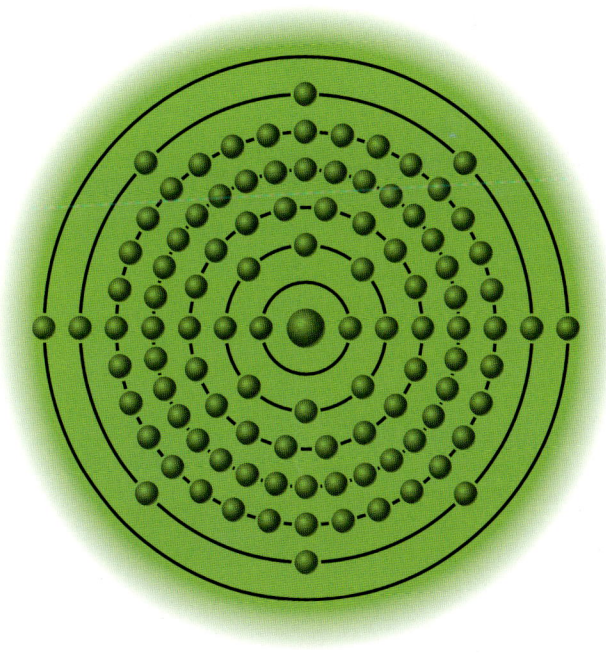

Discovery

It was possibly discovered by the Nobel Institute for Physics in Sweden in 1957 by bombarding curium with carbon ions. The official first authenticated discovery was made by Albert Ghiorso, T. Sikkeland, J. R. Walton and Glenn T. Seaborg at Berkeley, California, in 1958. This element is named after Alfred Bernhard Nobel, the Swedish inventor and philanthropist.

Technology

Because so little of it has been isolated, so far it has no uses.

Geology

It is an artificial element that does not occur in the environment.

Biology

Nobelium does not occur in living things; and because it is radioactive, if it were ever produced in substantial quantities, it has the potential to be harmful.

Osmium (Os)

Element 76. Osmium, a hard, brittle, grey-white metal, is the densest naturally occurring element. Osmium belongs to the transition metals in the Periodic Table.

It has a higher melting point than members of the platinum group. The solid metal is difficult to produce, but once made, it does not tarnish. The powdered form of the metal gives off a strong unpleasant smell. It was renowned for the unpleasantness (and poisonousness) of its odour.

Discovery

It was discovered by the English chemist Smithson Tennant in 1804.

Technology

Osmium is hard and brittle. It once was used for filaments in electric light bulbs, but it has now been replaced by tungsten. It now mainly makes an alloy for hardening platinum, especially in artificial body joints. An alloy of osmium and iridium is used in pen points. Osmium oxide powder helps detect fingerprints.

Geology

The native metal does not exist naturally, but an alloy called iridiosmium (a natural alloy of iridium and osmium) does exist. Otherwise, osmium is mainly found associated with platinum ores and with platinum-bearing sands.

Biology

Osmium does not occur in living things. Osmium salts, especially the tetroxide, are extremely dangerous if inhaled.

Key facts...

Name: osmium
Symbol: Os
Atomic number: 76
Atomic weight: 190.2
Position in Periodic Table: transition metal, group (8) (iron group); period 6. Precious metal
State at room temperature: solid
Colour: grey-white
Density of solid: 22.61 g/cc
Melting point: 3,033°C
Boiling point: 5,012°C
Origin of name: from the Greek word *osme*, meaning smell
Shell pattern of electrons: 2–8–18–32–14–2

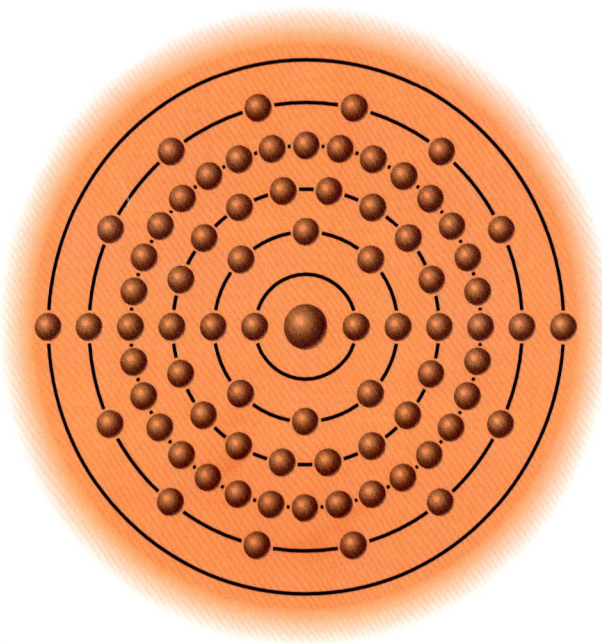

▼ Some pen points are made of an osmium and iridium alloy.

Oxygen (O)

Element 8. Oxygen is a non-metallic chemical element in group 6 (the oxygen group) in the Periodic Table.

Oxygen is the most common gas after nitrogen, making up just over one-fifth of the Earth's atmosphere. It is the third most abundant element in the universe after hydrogen and helium. It is a colourless, tasteless and odourless gas. When electrically excited, it produces colours. They are, for example, responsible for the bright red and yellow–green colours of an aurora in the night sky (northern or southern lights).

Oxygen is very reactive and reacts with many elements to produce oxides. The most common oxide is water.

Ozone (O_3) is a form of oxygen created when electrical discharges or ultra-violet light act on oxygen, O_2. Ozone is harmful if breathed in too large concentrations. High in the atmosphere, however, ozone prevents harmful ultra-violet rays from the Sun from reaching the Earth in too high a concentration. Ozone can be destroyed by reacting it with some gases.

Oxygen is essential for combustion, and spacecraft therefore have to take their own supply of liquid oxygen as well as fuel.

Oxygen is produced by liquefying air. Liquid oxygen is magnetic. High concentrations of oxygen present a fire hazard because of the increased risk of spontaneous combustion.

Key facts...
Name: oxygen
Symbol: O
Atomic number: 8
Atomic weight: 16
Position in Periodic Table: group 6 (16)
    (oxygen group; chalcogen); period 2
State at room temperature: gas
Colour: colourless as a gas, but pale blue as a liquid
Density of gas at 20°C: 1.33 g/l
Melting point: –218.3°C
Boiling point: –182.9°C
Origin of name: the French chemist Antoine
    Lavoisier gave oxygen its name, using
    the Greek words oxy and genes, meaning
    acid forming.
Shell pattern of electrons: 2–6

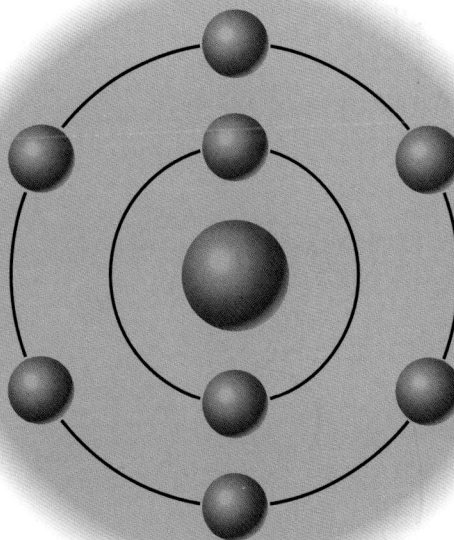

Oxygen group elements

Another term for the group 6 elements in the Periodic Table (also called the chalcogens). The members of the group are oxygen (O), sulphur (S), selenium (Se), tellurium (Te) and polonium (Po).

Discovery

Oxygen was discovered in 1772 by the Swedish chemist Carl Wilhelm Scheele. It was discovered independently by the English chemist Joseph Priestley in 1774. Because Priestley was the first to publish his findings, the discovery is usually attributed to him.

Technology

Oxygen is frequently used for combustion, such as in oxyacetylene welding. As a pure gas it can help people with breathing problems. In spacecraft it is part of the fuel system.

Geology

Oxygen makes up 89% by weight of sea water and 47% by weight of the Earth's crust.

Biology

Oxygen is vital for life. About two-thirds of the human body is oxygen. Animals take in oxygen and give out carbon dioxide. Plants take in carbon dioxide and give out oxygen. As a result, almost

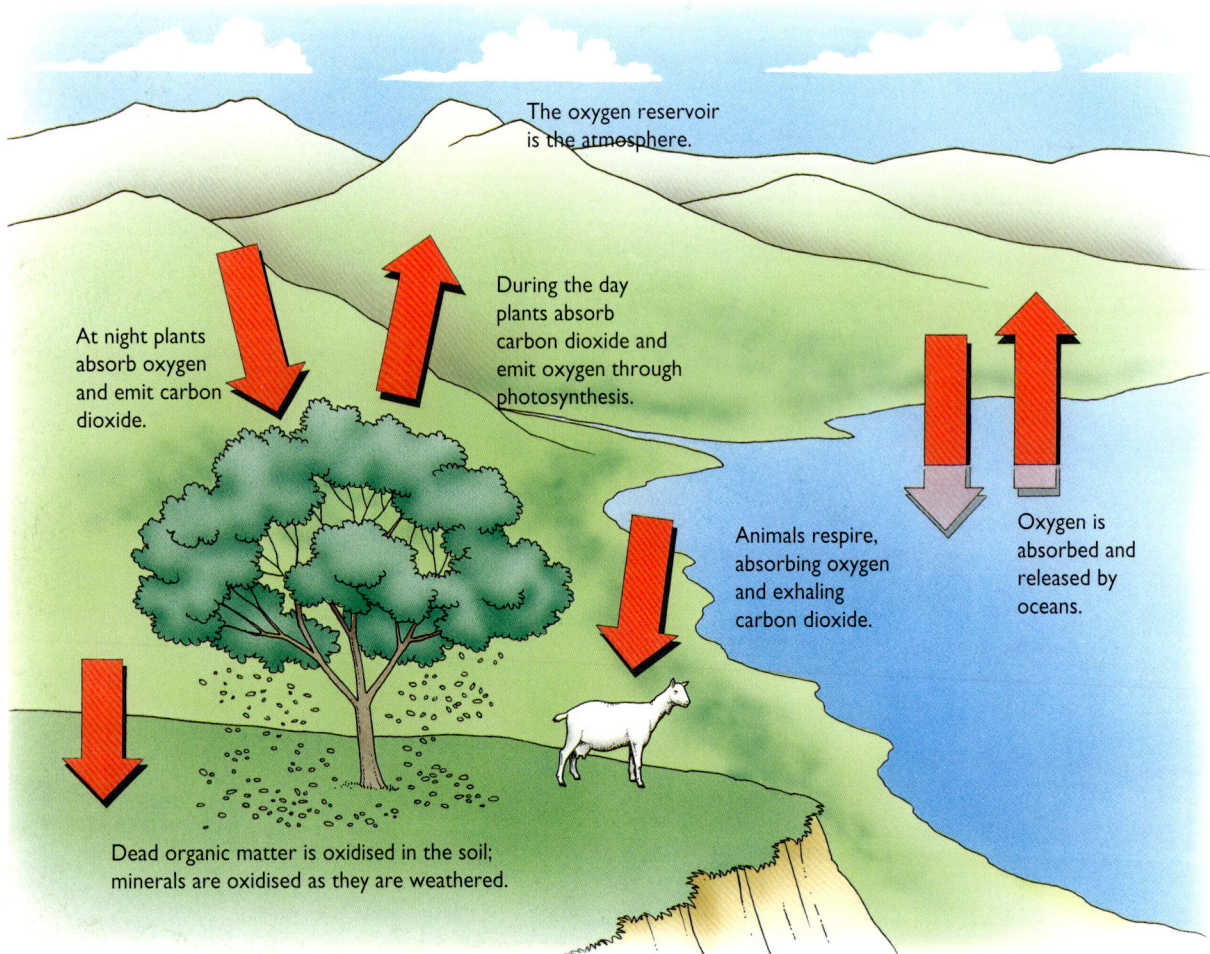

▼ The oxygen cycle.

The oxygen reservoir is the atmosphere.

During the day plants absorb carbon dioxide and emit oxygen through photosynthesis.

At night plants absorb oxygen and emit carbon dioxide.

Animals respire, absorbing oxygen and exhaling carbon dioxide.

Oxygen is absorbed and released by oceans.

Dead organic matter is oxidised in the soil; minerals are oxidised as they are weathered.

all of the oxygen in the atmosphere is from plants (the process is called photosynthesis). Some uncombined oxygen dissolves in water, providing the oxygen needed for marine animals.

▶ Oxygen being produced by aquatic plants.

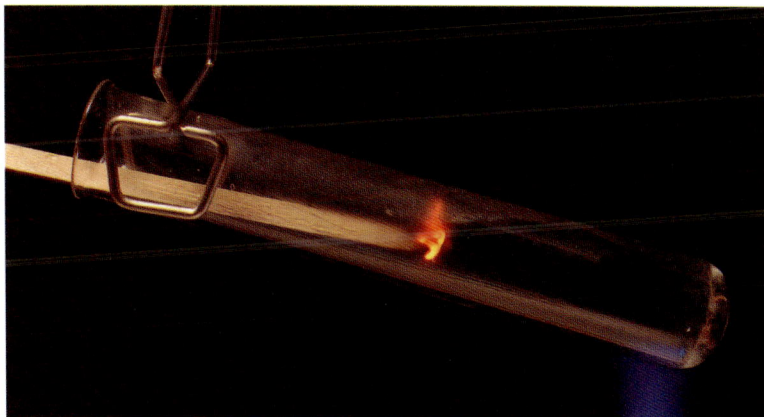

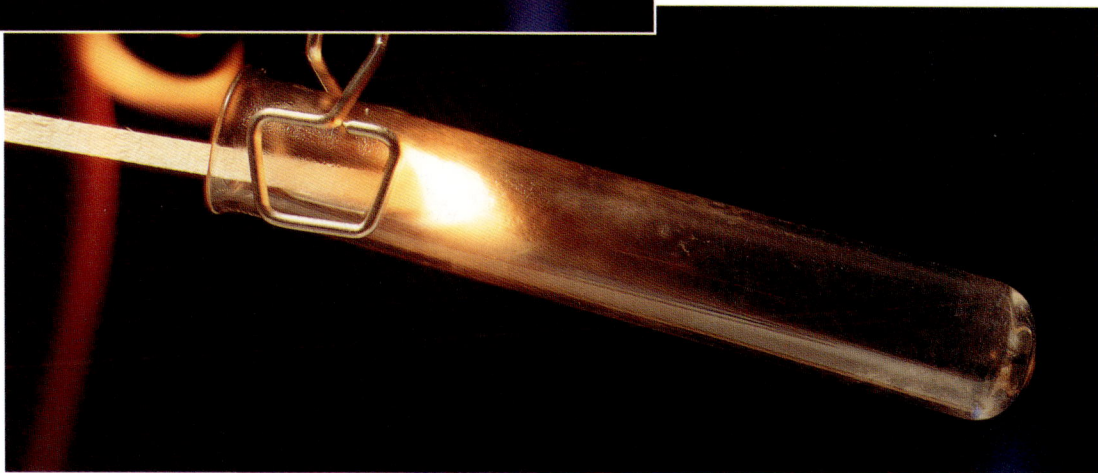

▲▶ When a glowing splint is introduced to a test tube containing oxygen, it will relight within a few seconds.

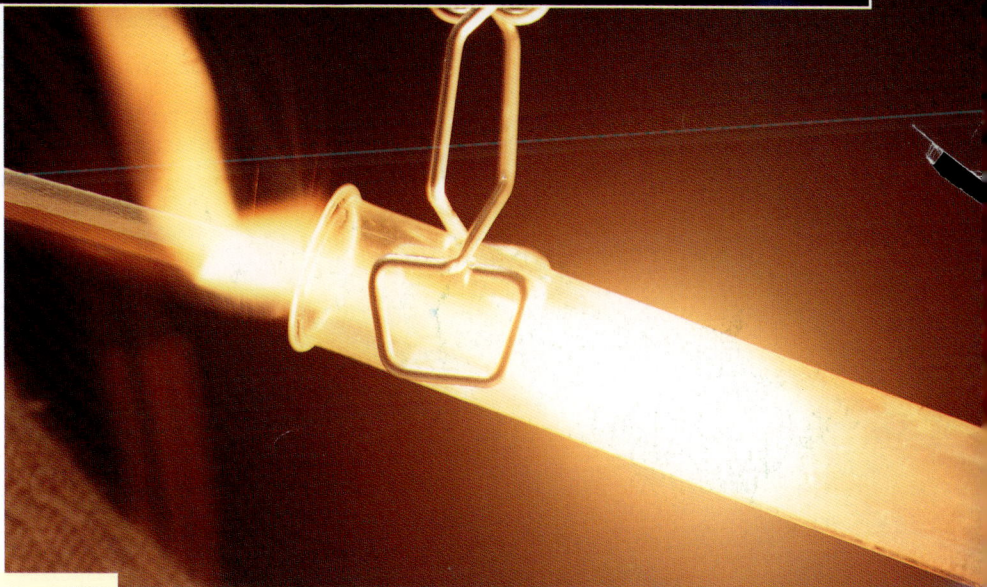

For more on oxygen, see Volume 12: Oxygen in the *Elements* set.

Palladium (Pd)

Element 46. This grey–white metal is a light transition metal in the Periodic Table. It does not corrode. It is the least dense and has the lowest melting point of the precious metals, which include platinum. It is soft and can be shaped unless it is cold worked, when it becomes hard. At room temperature palladium absorbs 900 times its own volume of hydrogen!

Discovery

Discovered by William Hyde Wollaston in England in 1803 in a sample of platinum ore.

Technology

It is used to increase the speed of chemical reactions (it is a catalyst). Because it does not corrode, palladium goes into electrical contacts to add reliability in telephone equipment. Some watch springs are made of palladium. Heated palladium helps purify hydrogen because hydrogen readily passes through it. Palladium is used as an alloy in jewellery. White gold is an alloy of gold decolourised by the addition of palladium that is used in crown dental work.

Geology

Palladium is found as a native metal in the same veins close to ancient volcanoes in which platinum, nickel, and copper appear. It is normally recovered as a by-product of refining these other metals.

Biology

Palladium is not found in living things.

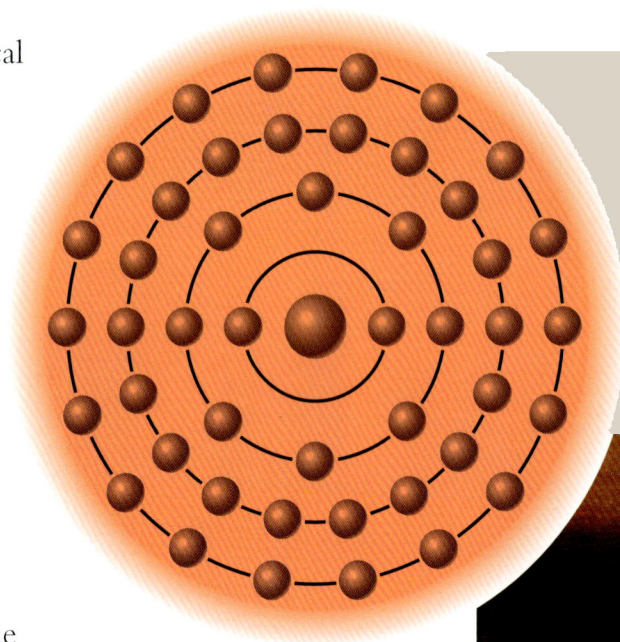

Phosphorus (P)

Element 15. Phosphorus is a member of group 5 (the nitrogen group) in the Periodic Table.

There are several forms of phosphorus: colourless, white, red and black. Most commonly it is a white, soft, waxy solid that is insoluble in water, that glows in the dark, is highly reactive in air and catches fire spontaneously. It turns into the red form when heated above 250°C or exposed to sunlight. Red phosphorus does not ignite spontaneously and so is less dangerous than white phosphorus. Black phosphorus is rare and only formed at high temperatures.

Key facts...

Name: phosphorus
Symbol: P
Atomic number: 15
Atomic weight: 30.97
Position in Periodic Table: group 5 (15) (nitrogen group); period 3
State at room temperature: solid
Colour: colourless, white, red, black
Density of solid: 1.82 g/cc (white)
Melting point: 44.2°C (white)
Boiling point: 280°C (white)
Origin of name: from the Greek word *phosphoros,* meaning bringer of light
Shell pattern of electrons: 2–8–5

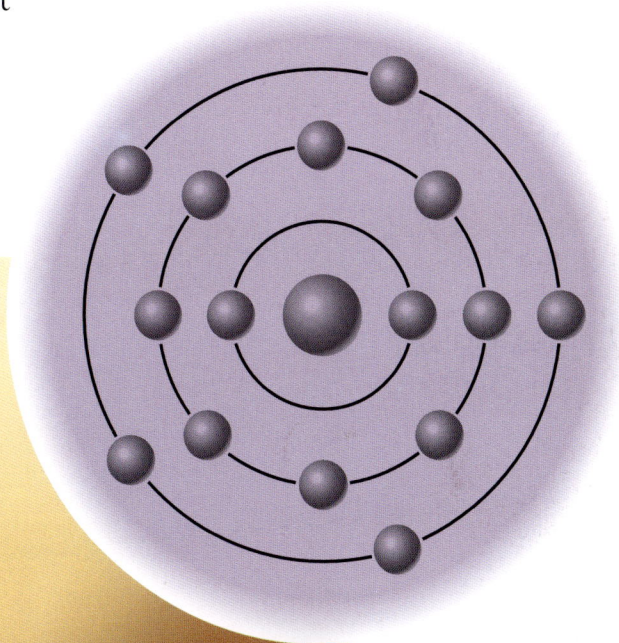

◄ These 'strike anywhere' matches contain a mixture of tetraphosphorus trisulphide (P_4S_3) and potassium chlorate ($KClO_3$). 'Safety' matches use potassium chlorate in the head of the match and red phosphorus in the striker on the matchbox side. The potassium chlorate provides the oxygen for the reaction.

Discovery

It was discovered by Hennig Brand in 1669 from the remains of evaporated urine. He boiled up more than 50 buckets of urine to get the result he needed.

Technology

White phosphorus has been used to make incendiary (burning) bombs. Red phosphorus is used for the striking surface of safety matches. Phosphorus compounds are widely applied in the manufacture of fertilisers. Phosphorus can also help make special steels and phosphor bronze. Sodium phosphate is a water softener and helps prevent corrosion of hot water systems.

◀▼ This standard chemistry demonstration uses phosphorus. White phosphorus ignites in the air in a bell jar, using up the oxygen during combustion. The water level rises, showing roughly the proportion of oxygen that was in the air.

Sticks of highly reactive white phosphorus.

When white phosphorus is heated in the absence of air, it changes to relatively unreactive red phosphorus.

Geology

Phosphorus is not found as the native element. It is extracted from phosphate ores. The main phosphate mineral is apatite (calcium phosphate, $CaPO_4$)

Biology

Phosphorus is present in all living cells, nerves, teeth, and bones. Exposure to phosphorus can lead to poisoning and the dissolving of the jaw (called phossy jaw).

For more on phosphorus, see Volume 11: Nitrogen and Phosphorus in the *Elements* set.

Platinum (Pt)

Element 78. Platinum is a soft, easily worked, and very heavy silvery-white metal. It is one of the transition metals in the Periodic Table.

Platinum has a high melting point and corrodes only very slowly in air, although it corrodes in the presence of alkalis. It is barely soluble in concentrated acids unless they are mixed together (as aqua regia). It is regarded as a precious metal. Platinum, like palladium, absorbs large volumes of hydrogen. It is also used as an agent to speed up chemical reactions (a catalyst). Hydrogen and oxygen gas mixtures explode in the presence of platinum wire. Platinum is a catalyst in the catalytic converters used in car exhausts.

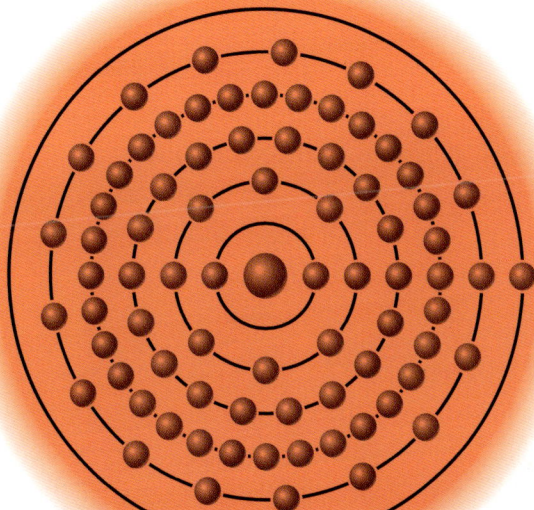

Key facts...

Name: platinum
Symbol: Pt
Atomic number: 78
Atomic weight: 195.08
Position in Periodic Table: transition metal, group (10), (nickel group); period 6. Precious metal
State at room temperature: solid
Colour: silvery-white
Density of solid: 21.45 g/cc
Melting point: 1,768.3°C
Boiling point: 3,825°C
Origin of name: the Spaniards found it in the river deposits of the Río Pinto, Colombia, and they named it *platina del Pinto* because it looked like silver.
Shell pattern of electrons: 2–8–18–32–17–1

Discovery

It was discovered by Julius Caesar Scaliger in 1557.

Technology

Platinum expands at the same rate as glassware, and so it is used to make electrodes for chemical apparatus. It also goes into jewellery and dental devices. Platinum anodes are used to protect ships, pipelines, and steel piers from salt water corrosion.

Geology

Platinum is found as a native metal in deposits near ancient volcanoes. It also occurs as platiniridium, a naturally occurring platinum–iridium alloy. It also occurs in sulphide ores as platinum sulphide, PtS.

Biology

Platinum is not found in living things.

Platinum electrodes are used for electrolysis in the laboratory because they are resistant to corrosion.

Plutonium (Pu)

Element 94. A radioactive element in the actinide series in the Periodic Table.

Amounts of more than about 300 grams are liable to explode spontaneously.

Key facts...

Name: plutonium
Symbol: Pu
Atomic number: 94
Atomic weight: 244
Position in Periodic Table: inner transition metal; period 7 (actinide series)
State at room temperature: solid
Colour: silvery-white
Density of solid: 19.84 g/cc
Melting point: 639.4°C
Boiling point: 3,235°C
Origin of name: named after the planet Pluto
Shell pattern of electrons: 2–8–18–32–24–8–2

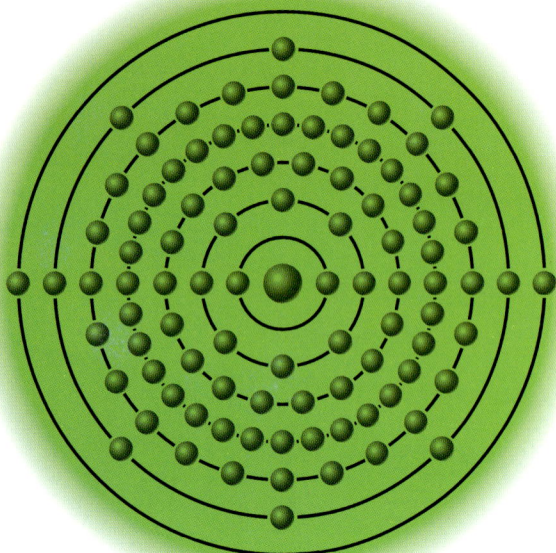

Discovery

It was discovered in 1940 by Glenn T. Seaborg, Joseph W. Kennedy and Arthur C. Wahl at Berkeley, California, through deuteron bombardment of uranium.

A nuclear power station

Technology

It is the most important of the transuranium elements because of its use in nuclear weapons and as a source of nuclear power. The isotope 239Pu has a half-life of more than 20,000 years. A kilogram of this isotope can release as much energy as about 22 million kilowatt–hours of heat from conventional power stations. A kilogram of plutonium produces an explosion equal to about 20,000 tonnes of TNT. Its long half–life makes spent plutonium difficult to dispose of.

Geology

Traces of plutonium are found in uranium ores, but most plutonium comes from the conversion of uranium in nuclear reactors. That is brought about by the absorption of neutrons. The result is a change from uranium-238 to uranium-239, which then decays to plutonium-239.

Biology

Plutonium is not found in living things and is a very dangerous radioactive element. Plutonium is particularly dangerous because it emits radiation that is absorbed by bone marrow.

For more on plutonium, see Volume 15: Uranium and Other Radioactive Elements in the *Elements* set.

Polonium (Po)

Element 84. Polonium is a radioactive, silvery-grey metalloid in group 6 (the oxygen group) in the Periodic Table. Polonium has more isotopes than any other element, all of which are radioactive.

Polonium was the first radioactive element to be discovered. It is one of the elements in the uranium–radium series of radioactive decay. Natural polonium is a very rare element.

Discovery

It was discovered in 1898 by Pierre and Marie Curie while they were looking for the cause of radioactivity in pitchblende. Marie had to grind up many tonnes of pitchblende just to get a few tenths of a gram of polonium. She named the element after her native country, Poland.

In 1934 scientists discovered they could obtain the parent of polonium if they

bombarded natural bismuth with neutrons. That is how it is now prepared, and synthetic polonium is available in commercial quantities.

Technology

Polonium is a good source of alpha radiation because its isotopes disintegrate by emitting alpha particles. It is used as a source of neutrons and in devices that ionise air in order to reduce electrostatic charge.

Geology

It is found in very tiny amounts in uranium and radium ores. It is obtained as a by-product of radium extraction during uranium ore refining.

Biology

Polonium is not part of living things. However, it is highly radioactive and therefore dangerous to people unless they are protected from it. It emits alpha rays, but these are quite easily shielded using gold foil. That is why it can be used in factories for reducing static electricity.

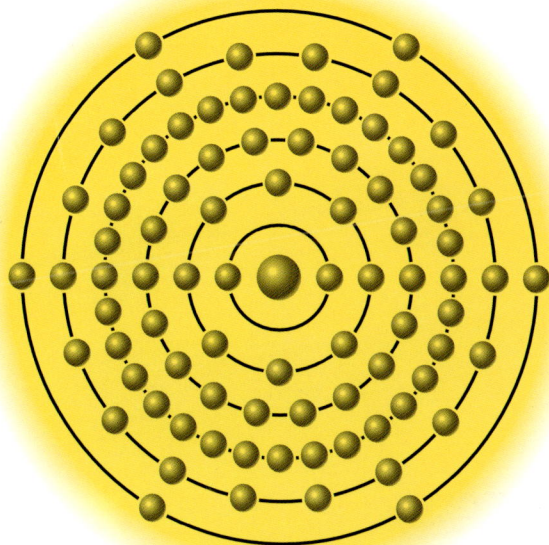

Key facts...
Name: polonium
Symbol: Po
Atomic number: 84
Atomic weight: 209
Position in Periodic Table: group 6 (16) (oxygen group; chalcogen); period 6
State at room temperature: solid
Colour: silvery-grey
Density of solid: 9.4 g/cc
Melting point: 254°C
Boiling point: 962°C
Origin of name: named after Poland, the birthplace of Marie Curie
Shell pattern of electrons: 2–8–18–32–18–6

The Periodic Table

Actinium (Ac)	89	Calcium (Ca)	20	Fermium (Fm)	100
Aluminium (Al)	13	Californium (Cf)	98	Fluorine (F)	9
Antimony (Sb)	51	Carbon (C)	6	Francium (Fr)	87
Americium (Am)	95	Cerium (Ce)	58	Gadolinium (Gd)	64
Argon (Ar)	18	Cesium (Cs)	55	Gallium (Ga)	31
Arsenic (As)	33	Chlorine (Cl)	17	Germanium (Ge)	32
Astatine (At)	85	Chromium (Cr)	24	Gold (Au)	79
Barium (Ba)	56	Cobalt (Co)	27	Hafnium (Hf)	72
Berkelium (Bk)	97	Copper (Cu)	29	Hassium (Hs)	108
Beryllium (Be)	4	Curium (Cm)	96	Helium (He)	2
Bismuth (Bi)	83	Dubnium (Db)	105	Holmium (Ho)	67
Bohrium (Bh)	107	Dysprosium (Dy)	66	Hydrogen (H)	1
Boron (B)	5	Einsteinium (Es)	99	Indium (In)	49
Bromine (Br)	35	Erbium (Er)	68	Iodine (I)	53
Cadmium (Cd)	48	Europium (Eu)	63	Iridium (Ir)	77

GROUPS ▶

PERIODS ▼

Transition metals

Group	1 (1)	2 (2)	(3)	(4)	(5)	(6)	(7)	(8)
Period 1	1 **H** Hydrogen 1							
Period 2	3 **Li** Lithium 7	4 **Be** Beryllium 9						
Period 3	11 **Na** Sodium 23	12 **Mg** Magnesium 24						
Period 4	19 **K** Potassium 39	20 **Ca** Calcium 40	21 **Sc** Scandium 45	22 **Ti** Titanium 48	23 **V** Vanadium 51	24 **Cr** Chromium 52	25 **Mn** Manganese 55	26 **Fe** Iron 56
Period 5	37 **Rb** Rubidium 85	38 **Sr** Strontium 88	39 **Y** Yttrium 89	40 **Zr** Zirconium 91	41 **Nb** Niobium 93	42 **Mo** Molybdenum 96	43 **Tc** Technetium (99)	44 **Ru** Ruthenium 101
Period 6	55 **Cs** Cesium 133	56 **Ba** Barium 137	71 **Lu** Lutetium 175	72 **Hf** Hafnium 178	73 **Ta** Tantalum 181	74 **W** Tungsten 184	75 **Re** Rhenium 186	76 **Os** Osmium 190
Period 7	87 **Fr** Francium (223)	88 **Ra** Radium (226)	103 **Lr** Lawrencium (260)	104 **Rf** Rutherfordium (261)	105 **Db** Dubnium (262)	106 **Sg** Seaborgium (263)	107 **Bh** Bohrium (262)	108 **Hs** Hassium (265)

- Metals
- Metalloids (semi-metals)
- Non-metals
- Inner transition metals

Lanthanide series

57 **La** Lanthanum 139	58 **Ce** Cerium 140	59 **Pr** Praseodymium 141	60 **Nd** Neodymium 144

Actinide series

89 **Ac** Actinium (227)	90 **Th** Thorium (232)	91 **Pa** Protactinium (231)	92 **U** Uranium (238)

Iron (Fe) 26	Neptunium (Np) 93	Protactinium (Pa) 91	Strontium (Sr) 38	Ununoctium (Uuo) 118
Krypton (Kr) 36	Nickel (Ni) 28	Radium (Ra) 88	Sulphur (S) 16	Ununquadium (Uuq) 114
Lanthanum (La) 57	Niobium (Nb) 41	Radon (Rn) 86	Tantalum (Ta) 73	Unununium (Uuu) 111
Lawrencium (Lr) 103	Nitrogen (N) 7	Rhenium (Re) 75	Technetium (Tc) 43	Uranium (U) 92
Lead (Pb) 82	Nobelium (No) 102	Rhodium (Rh) 45	Tellurium (Te) 52	Vanadium (V) 23
Lithium (Li) 3	Osmium (Os) 76	Rubidium (Rb) 37	Terbium (Tb) 65	Xenon (Xe) 54
Lutetium (Lu) 71	Oxygen (O) 8	Ruthenium (Ru) 44	Thallium (Tl) 81	Ytterbium (Yb) 70
Magnesium (Mg) 12	Palladium (Pd) 46	Rutherfordium (Rf) 104	Thorium (Th) 90	Yttrium (Y) 39
Manganese (Mn) 25	Phosphorus (P) 15	Samarium (Sm) 62	Thulium (Tm) 69	Zinc (Zn) 30
Meitnerium (Mt) 109	Platinum (Pt) 78	Scandium (Sc) 27	Tin (Sn) 50	Zirconium (Zr) 40
Mendelevium (Md) 101	Plutonium (Pu) 94	Seaborgium (Sg) 106	Titanium (Ti) 22	
Mercury (Hg) 80	Polonium (Po) 84	Selenium (Se) 34	Tungsten (W) 74	
Molybdenum (Mo) 42	Potassium (K) 19	Silicon (Si) 14	Ununbium (Uub) 112	
Neodymium (Nd) 60	Praseodymium (Pr) 59	Silver (Ag) 47	Ununhexium (Uuh) 116	
Neon (Ne) 10	Promethium (Pm) 61	Sodium (Na) 11	Ununnilium (Uun) 110	

				3	**4**	**5**	**6**	**7**	**8 or 0**
(9)	(10)	(11)	(12)	(13)	(14)	(15)	(16)	(17)	(18)
									2 **He** Helium 4
				5 **B** Boron 11	6 **C** Carbon 12	7 **N** Nitrogen 14	8 **O** Oxygen 16	9 **F** Fluorine 19	10 **Ne** Neon 20
				13 **Al** Aluminium 27	14 **Si** Silicon 28	15 **P** Phosphorus 31	16 **S** Sulphur 32	17 **Cl** Chlorine 35	18 **Ar** Argon 40
27 **Co** Cobalt 59	28 **Ni** Nickel 59	29 **Cu** Copper 64	30 **Zn** Zinc 65	31 **Ga** Gallium 70	32 **Ge** Germanium 73	33 **As** Arsenic 75	34 **Se** Selenium 79	35 **Br** Bromine 80	36 **Kr** Krypton 84
45 **Rh** Rhodium 103	46 **Pd** Palladium 106	47 **Ag** Silver 108	48 **Cd** Cadmium 112	49 **In** Indium 115	50 **Sn** Tin 119	51 **Sb** Antimony 122	52 **Te** Tellurium 128	53 **I** Iodine 127	54 **Xe** Xenon 131
77 **Ir** Iridium 192	78 **Pt** Platinum 195	79 **Au** Gold 197	80 **Hg** Mercury 201	81 **Tl** Thallium 204	82 **Pb** Lead 207	83 **Bi** Bismuth 209	84 **Po** Polonium (209)	85 **At** Astatine (210)	86 **Rn** Radon (222)
109 **Mt** Meitnerium (266)	110 **Uun** Ununnilium (272)	111 **Uuu** Unununium (272)	112 **Uub** Ununbium (277)		114 **Uuq** Ununquadium (289)		116 **Uuh** Ununhexium (289)		118 **Uuo** Ununoctium (293)

61 **Pm** Promethium (145)	62 **Sm** Samarium 150	63 **Eu** Europium 152	64 **Gd** Gadolinium 157	65 **Tb** Terbium 159	66 **Dy** Dysprosium 163	67 **Ho** Holmium 165	68 **Er** Erbium 167	69 **Tm** Thulium 169	70 **Yb** Ytterbium 173
93 **Np** Neptunium (237)	94 **Pu** Plutonium (244)	95 **Am** Americium (243)	96 **Cm** Curium (247)	97 **Bk** Berkelium (247)	98 **Cf** Californium (251)	99 **Es** Einsteinium (252)	100 **Fm** Fermium (257)	101 **Md** Mendelevium (258)	102 **No** Nobelium (259)

Understanding equations

As you read through Volumes 1 to 15 in the Elements set, you will notice that many pages contain equations using symbols. Symbols make it easy for chemists to write out the reactions that are occurring in a way that allows a better understanding of the processes involved. If you are not familiar with these symbols, these pages explain them.

Symbols for the elements

The basis for the modern use of symbols for elements dates back to the 19th century. At that time a shorthand was developed using the first letter of the element wherever possible.

Thus O stands for oxygen, H stands for hydrogen, and so on. However, if we were to use only the first letter, there could be some confusion. For example, nitrogen and nickel would both use the symbols N. To overcome this problem, many element symbols take the first two letters of the full name, with the second letter in lower case. So, although nitrogen is N, nickel becomes Ni. Not all symbols come from the English name; many use the Latin name instead. That is why, for example, gold is not G but Au (from the Latin *aurum*), and sodium has the symbol Na (from the Latin *natrium*).

Compounds of elements are made by combining letters. So, the molecule carbon

Written and symbolic equations

In this book important chemical equations are briefly stated in words (they are called word equations) and are then shown in their symbolic form along with the states.

What reaction the equation illustrates

EQUATION: The formation of calcium hydroxide

Word equation —————— *Calcium oxide + water ⇨ calcium hydroxide*

Symbol equation ————— $CaO(s)$ + $H_2O(l)$ ⇨ $Ca(OH)_2(aq)$

heated

Sometimes you will find additional descriptions below the symbolic equation.

Symbol showing the state: s is for solid, l is for liquid, g is for gas, and aq is for aqueous.

Diagrams

Some of the equations are shown as graphic representations.

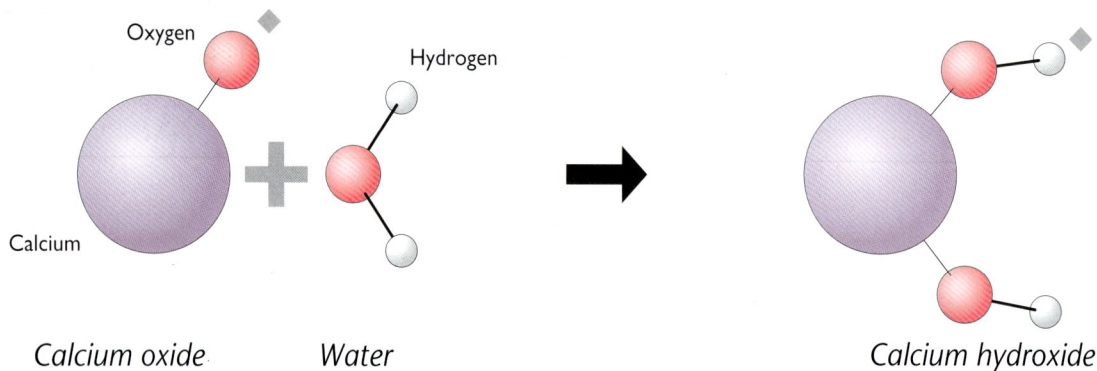

Oxygen

Hydrogen

Calcium

Calcium oxide   Water

Calcium hydroxide

Sometimes the written equation is broken up and put below the relevant stages in the graphic representation.

monoxide is CO. By using lowercase letters for the second letter of an element, it is possible to show that cobalt, symbol Co, is not the same as the molecule carbon monoxide, CO.

However, the letters can be made to do much more than this. In many molecules atoms combine in unequal numbers. So, for example, carbon dioxide has one atom of carbon for every two of oxygen. That is shown by using the number 2 beside the oxygen, and the symbol becomes CO_2.

In practice, some groups of atoms combine as a unit with other substances. Thus, for example, calcium bicarbonate (one of the compounds used in some antacid pills) is written $Ca(HCO_3)_2$. This shows that the part of the substance inside the parentheses reacts as a unit, and the 2 outside the parentheses shows the presence of two such units.

Some substances attract water molecules to themselves. To show this, a dot is used. So, the blue form of copper sulphate is written $CuSO_4.5H_2O$. In this case five molecules of water are attracted to one of copper sulphate. When you see the dot, you know that this water can be driven off by heating; it is part of the crystal structure.

In a reaction substances change by rearranging the combinations of atoms. The way in which they change is shown by using the chemical symbols, placing those that will react (the starting materials, or reactants) on the left and the products of the reaction on the right. Between the two an arrow shows which way the reaction is going.

It is possible to describe a reaction in words. That produces word equations, which are given throughout Volumes 1 to 15. However, it is easier to understand what is happening by using an equation containing symbols. They are also given in many places. They are not shown when the equations are very complex.

In any equation both sides balance; that is, there must be an equal number of like atoms on both sides of the arrow. When you try to write down reactions, you, too, must balance your equation; you cannot have a few atoms left over at the end!

The symbols in parentheses are abbreviations for the physical state of each substance taking part, so that (*s*) is used for solid, (*l*) for liquid, (*g*) for gas, and (*aq*) for an aqueous solution, that is, a solution of a substance dissolved in water.

Atoms and ions
Each sphere represents a particle of an element. A particle can be an atom or an ion. Each atom or ion is associated with other atoms or ions through bonds – forces of attraction. The size of the particles and the nature of the bonds can be extremely important in determining the nature of the reaction or the properties of the compound.

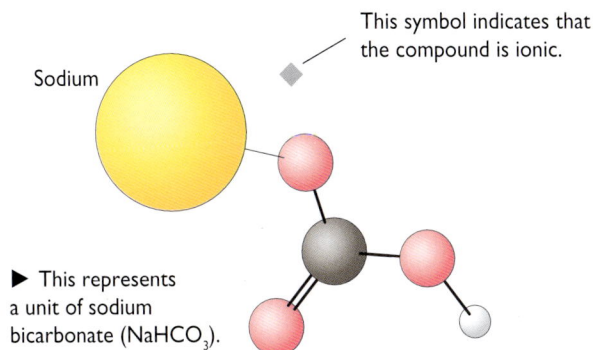

This symbol indicates that the compound is ionic.

Sodium

▶ This represents a unit of sodium bicarbonate ($NaHCO_3$).

The term "unit" is sometimes used to simplify the representation of a combination of ions.

Chemical symbols, equations and diagrams
The arrangement of any molecule or compound can be shown in one of the two ways shown below, depending on which gives the clearer picture. The left-hand image is called a ball-and-stick diagram because it uses rods and spheres to show the structure of the material. This example shows water, H_2O. There are two hydrogen atoms and one oxygen atom.

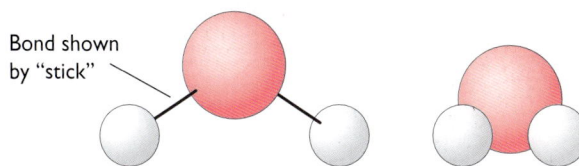

Bond shown by "stick"

Colours too
The colours of each of the particles help differentiate the elements involved. The diagram can then be matched to the written and symbolic equation given with the diagram. In the case above, oxygen is red, and hydrogen is grey.

Set Index

USING THE SET INDEX

The 18 volumes in the *Elements* set are:

Volume Number   *Title*

1. Hydrogen and the Noble Gases
2. Sodium and Potassium
3. Calcium and Magnesium
4. Iron, Chromium and Manganese
5. Copper, Silver and Gold
6. Zinc, Cadmium and Mercury
7. Aluminium
8. Carbon
9. Silicon
10. Lead and Tin
11. Nitrogen and Phosphorus
12. Oxygen
13. Sulphur
14. Chlorine, Fluorine, Bromine and Iodine
15. Uranium and Other Radioactive Elements
16. Actinium to Fluorine
17. Francium to Polonium
18. Potassium to Zirconium

An example entry:

Index entries are listed alphabetically. Volume numbers are in bold and are followed by page references in roman.

sodium (Na) **See Vol. 2 and Vol. 18:** 24–25; **1:** 36, **7:** 6, **9:** 11, 24, 38

In this case sodium gets extensive coverage in Volume 2: Sodium and Potassium and on pages 24 and 25 of Volume 18: Potassium to Zirconium. Sodium is also discussed on page 36 of Volume 1, page 6 of Volume 7, and pages 11, 24 and 38 of Volume 9.

A

A-bomb **15:** 38
Ac *see* actinium
acetate **8:** 41
acetic acid **1:** 31, **7:** 33, **8:** 29
acetone **7:** 34, **8:** 28
acetylene **8:** 29, **14:** 22
acid **1:** 12, 18, 19, 20, 22, 23, 34, 35, 36, 37, **2:** 31, **3:** 12, 21, 29, 39, 42, **7:** 14, 33, **13:** 19, 26, 27
acid burn **1:** 24, **13:** 26, **2:** 32, 33, **3:** 13, **4:** 10, **7:** 40, 42, 43, **10:** 12, **11:** 31, 32, **12:** 13, 29, 42, **13:** 18, 19, 22, 23
acidity **1:** 20–21
acidosis **1:** 28
acids **9:** 11
acid soil **4:** 17
actinides, actinide series **16:** 8 *see also* Periodic Table
actinium (Ac) **16:** 17
activated charcoal **8:** 22, 23, **14:** 27
addition polymer **8:** 32–35

adhesive **3:** 22, 23, **12:** 20
admiralty brass **5:** 18
adsorption **14:** 27, **7:** 35, **8:** 23
aeration **12:** 8, 9
aeroembolism **11:** 7
Ag *see* silver
agate **9:** 13, 14
Agent Orange **14:** 29
air **11:** 38, **12:** 6, 7, 17
air bag **11:** 29
Al *see* aluminium
alchemists, alchemy **1:** 22, 23, **15:** 11
alclad **7:** 23
alcohols **8:** 28
algae **3:** 4, 40, **11:** 43
algal blooms **11:** 43
alkali **1:** 20, 34, 35, **2:** 5, 32, **7:** 14, 33, 36, **11:** 12, 14, 15, 39
alkaline **1:** 20, 32, 33, **2:** 6, 31, 32
alkanes (paraffins) **8:** 28
alloy **4:** 34, 35, 36–37, 40, **5:** 20, **6:** 20, 22, 41, **7:** 22–23, **9:** 31, **10:** 40, 41
alpha particle **15:** 8, 42
alpha radiation **15:** 8, 9
alum **7:** 4, 7, 36, **8:** 15
alumina **7:** 16, 17, 18, 19, 34
alumina-silica gel **8:** 27, **1:** 26, 36
aluminium (Al) **See Vol. 7 and Vol. 16:** 18–19; **1:** 26, 36, **2:** 32, **4:** 22, 23, **5:** 21, 35, **6:** 22, **9:** 11, 20, 26, 34, 37, **10:** 39, **11:** 37, **12:** 10, 38, **15:** 9
aluminium foil **7:** 21, 30
aluminium hydroxide **7:** 36, 37, 38
aluminium oxide **7:** 4, 14, 16, 17, 18, 34, 35, **8:** 20, 21, **9:** 13, **12:** 11, 39, **4:** 17
aluminium silicate **9:** 26
aluminium sulphate **7:** 7, 36, 38, **8:** 15
Am *see* americium
amalgam **5:** 35, 42, **6:** 26, 36, 37, **7:** 22, **14:** 19
amalgamation **5:** 39
Amatol **11:** 27
americium (Am) **16:** 21
amethyst **9:** 12
amino acids **8:** 36
ammonia **1:** 16–17, 22, 26, 27, 32, **2:** 28, 29, **7:** 36, **11:** 12–17, 36, 37, **13:** 36, 43, **14:** 17, 34, 39
ammonia fountain **11:** 15
ammonia solution **5:** 27
ammonite **3:** 9
ammonium chloride **1:** 22, 23, **2:** 28, 29, **4:** 41, **6:** 14, 15, **11:** 13, **14:** 34
ammonium dichromate **11:** 24, 25
ammonium hydroxide **11:** 12
ammonium nitrate **11:** 13, 27
ammonium nitrite **11:** 27
ammonium perchlorate **12:** 39, **14:** 24
ammonium sulphate **7:** 36, **11:** 14, **13:** 43

ammunition **10:** 15, **11:** 27
amorphous **9:** 38
amphiboles **9:** 24
amphoteric **6:** 10, **7:** 14
anaesthetics **14:** 5
anglesite **10:** 7
anhydrous **13:** 34
anions **3:** 29, 6: 12,
annealing **7:** 20, **9:** 41
anode **2:** 23, 26, **3:** 37, **6:** 12, 13, **7:** 19, 25, **10:** 11
anodising **7:** 26
antacid **2:** 31, **3:** 5, 42, 47, **8:** 15
anthracite **8:** 7
antibacterial agent **6:** 38
antimony (Sb) **See Vol. 16:** 20; **10:** 15, 40
antimony-133 **15:** 29
antioxidant **11:** 10
antiseptic **14:** 41
apatite **11:** 42
approximate relative atomic mass **16:** 7
aqua fortis **1:** 26, **11:** 36
aqua regia **1:** 22, 26, **5:** 41, **11:** 36
aquamarine **9:** 23, **12:** 10
aquifers **2:** 20
architectural brass **5:** 19
Ar *see* argon
argon (Ar) **See Vol. 1 and Vol. 16:** 22; **4:** 30, **11:** 8, 9, **12:** 17, **15:** 11
arsenic (As) **See Vol. 16:** 23; **2:** 30, **13:** 42
As *see* arsenic
asbestos **14:** 20
asphalt **8:** 26, 27
aspirin **1:** 30
astatine (At) **16:** 24
At *see* astatine
atmosphere **3:** 12, **11:** 6, **12:** 6, 8, 12
atom, atoms **1–15:** 47, **16–18:** 57; **1:** 4, 38, **8:** 8, **15:** 4, 7, **16:** 4, 11
atomic bomb **15:** 38, 39
atomic mass **16:** 15 *see also* approximate relative atomic mass
atomic number **16:** 4, 7, 15
atomic weight **16:** 15
Au *see* gold
augite **9:** 24
aurora **12:** 7, **11:** 7
Australia **7:** 11
azide **11:** 29

B

B *see* boron
Ba *see* barium
background radiation **15:** 14–15
Bacon, Roger **11:** 26
bacteria **13:** 8, 20
Baekeland, Leo **8:** 31
Bakelite **8:** 31
baking powder **2:** 30
baking soda **2:** 28, 30, **8:** 14
barite **13:** 12, **16:** 24, 25
barium (Ba) **16:** 25
barium chlorate **14:** 24
barium-142 **15:** 28
barium peroxide **4:** 22
barium sulphate **13:** 12
barometer **6:** 30

basalt **9:** 24, 43, **15:** 18
base **1:** 22, 23, 32–33, 34, **2:** 32, **3:** 21, 25
base bullion **10:** 10
basic-oxygen furnace process **4:** 30, 31
basic-oxygen process **12:** 27
battery **4:** 41, **6:** 5, 12, **10:** 28, **13:** 30, 31
bauxite **7:** 10–11, 13, 14, 16, 18
Bayer, Karl Joseph **7:** 12
Bayer process **7:** 14, 16
Be *see* beryllium
becquerel **15:** 13, 22
Becquerel, A. H. **6:** 35, **15:** 5, 12, 22
bell-making bronze **5:** 21
bends **11:** 7
Benin bronze **5:** 19
benzene ring **8:** 33
berkelium (Bk) **16:** 26
beryl **7:** 8, **9:** 22
beryllium (Be) **See Vol. 16:** 27; **7:** 8, **9:** 22
Bessemer Converter **4:** 31, **12:** 27
Bessemer, Sir Henry **4:** 31
beta particle **15:** 8
beta radiation **15:** 8, 9
Bh *see* bohrium
Bi *see* bismuth
bicarbonate **1:** 29, 31
Big Bang **15:** 7
biotite **7:** 6, **9:** 26
bismuth (Bi) **See Vol. 16:** 28; **10:** 11
Bk *see* berkelium
black phosphorus **11:** 38
blast furnace **4:** 24, 25, 26, 27, **12:** 26
bleach **4:** 42, **12:** 21, **13:** 18, 20–21, **14:** 14, 15, 24
bleaching agent **13:** 18–21
blood **12:** 15
blood (salts) **2:** 18, 19
blue–green algae **11:** 18, 19, 22
Blue John **14:** 8, 36
blue vitriol **5:** 24, **13:** 32
body **2:** 18,19, **3:** 5, 32
bog iron ore **4:** 13
bohrium (Bh) **16:** 29
bond **1:** 9, 11, **2:** 23, **3:** 47
bone **3:** 5, 32
Bordeaux mixture **5:** 23, **13:** 34, 42
bornite **5:** 6
boron (B) **16:** 30
boron oxide **9:** 38
borosilicate glass **9:** 39, **16:** 30
Br *see* bromine
brass **5:** 18–19, 20, 27, **6:** 4, 20, **10:** 15
braze **5:** 18, **7:** 20
Brazil **7:** 11
breeder reactor **15:** 35
brimstone **13:** 4, 5, 10
brimstone and treacle **13:** 42
brine **1:** 14, 15, **2:** 12, 13, 25, 26, 27, 28, 29, 40, **6:** 33, **14:** 18, 19, 20
bromide **14:** 4
bromine (Br) **See Vol. 14 and Vol. 16:** 31; **8:** 23
bromothymol blue **1:** 21
bronze **5:** 20–21, 27, 34, **6:** 20, 21, **10:** 40, 41

Bronze Age **5:** 20, **10:** 5, 41
buckled ring **13:** 6
buckminsterfullerene **8:** 8, 22
buffer **1:** 28, 29
building stone **3:** 18
burette **1:** 35
burnt lime **3:** 22
burnt ochre **4:** 13
butane **8:** 7, 26, 28

C

C *see* carbon
Ca *see* calcium
cadmium (Cd) **See Vol. 6 and
   Vol. 16:** 32; **15:** 34
cadmium battery **6:** 41
cadmium borate **6:** 42
cadmium hydroxide **6:** 41
cadmium plating **6:** 40
cadmium sulphide **6:** 40, 42, 43,
   9: 41, **13:** 12, 24, 25
cadmium telluride **6:** 42
cadmium test **6:** 40
caesium *see* cesium
calcite **3:** 8, 10, 14, 16, 33, **9:** 18
calcium (Ca) **See Vol. 3 and Vol.
   16:** 33–34; **7:** 6, **9:** 11, 20, 38
calcium bicarbonate **1:** 29, **3:** 15,
   27, 38, 42
calcium carbonate **1:** 23, 29, 34,
   3: 4, 8, 12, 15, 16, 21, 26, 33,
   39, 43, **4:** 31, **8:** 15, **9:** 9, 18,
   39, 40, **14:** 35
calcium chlorate **14:** 14, 16, 24
calcium chloride **2:** 28, **14:** 19
calcium fluoride **3:** 8, **14:** 8, 9
calcium hydrogen carbonate **3:** 38
calcium hydroxide **3:** 6, 24, 26, 28,
   11: 14
calcium ions **3:** 25, 28, 40,
calcium oxide **2:** 29, **3:** 20, 24, 46,
   4: 26, 31, **7:** 16, **11:** 14,
   12: 26, **14:** 14
calcium phosphate **3:** 32, **11:** 38,
   42, 43, **14:** 37
calcium silicate **4:** 26
calcium sulphate **3:** 8, 30, **4:** 25,
   13: 9, 12, 13, 32, **11:** 43
californium (Cf) **16:** 35
calomel **6:** 32
camphor **8:** 31
cancer **15:** 42
cans **7:** 32, 33, 40
carats **5:** 40
carbohydrate **8:** 18
carbon (C) **See Vol. 8 and Vol.
   16:** 10, 13, 36–37; **1:** 24,
   4: 27, 28, 29, 30, 31, 32, 34,
   41, **6:** 14, 15, **7:** 18, 19,
   9: 31, **10:** 8, 10, **12:** 24, 26,
   13: 26, 27, **14:** 13, 15, **15:** 7
carbon black **4:** 41, **8:** 22
carbon compounds **8:** 6
carbon cycle **8:** 10–11, 13
carbon dating **15:** 18
carbon dioxide **1:** 23, 28, **2:** 28, 29,
   30, 31, **3:** 12, 19, 26, 43, 47,
   4: 26, 27, **7:** 38, 39, **8:** 10,
   11, 12–15, 18, **11:** 8, **12:** 14,
   15, 24, 38, 41
carbon dioxide, radioactive **15:** 14
carbon-14 **11:** 6, **15:** 7, 10, 16,
   17, 19

carbonic acid **1:** 28–29, **3:** 12
Carboniferous Period **8:** 7
carbon monoxide **4:** 24, 27, 30,
   5: 8, 9, **6:** 8, **8:** 16 17, **10:** 8,
   12: 13, 24
carbon rod **4:** 41
carbon tetrachloride **14:** 30
carbon-12 **15:** 7
carbonyl compounds **8:** 28
carborundum **8:** 5
carboxylic acid **1:** 30
carnellian **9:** 13
case hardening **4:** 33
cassiterite **10:** 34
cast iron **4:** 24, 28, 29
casting **6:** 22, 23, **7:** 22
Castner, Hamilton **2:** 26
Castner–Kellner cell **6:** 33
Castner–Kellner process **14:** 18–19
catalyst **1:** 12, 13, 17, **8:** 27, **11:** 17,
   13: 22, 28
catalytic converter **12:** 41, **8:** 16,
   10: 33
cathode **2:** 23, 27, **3:** 37, **4:** 41,
   6: 12, 13, **7:** 18, 19, **10:** 11
cathode ray tube **6:** 42
cathodic protection **4:** 7, 32, 33,
   12: 32, 33
cathodic protector **7:** 25
cation **2:** 15, 35, **3:** 29
cat's-eye **9:** 13
caustic **3:** 22
caustic soda **1:** 32, **2:** 6, 32, 34, 35,
   7: 15
caves, cave formations and caverns
   3: 14
Cd *see* cadmium
Ce *see* cerium
cell **6:** 13
cellulose **8:** 18, 31, 38, **12:** 14
cellulose acetate **8:** 31
cellulose nitrate **8:** 31
cement **3:** 5, 21, 22, **9:** 18
ceramic **9:** 29, 31
cerise **10:** 30
cerium (Ce) **16:** 38
cerussite **10:** 7
cesium (Cs) **16:** 39
cesium-137 **15:** 39
Cf *see* californium
CFCs *see* chlorofluorocarbons
chain silicates **9:** 24
chalcedony **9:** 13
chalcopyrite **5:** 6, **13:** 12
chalk **3:** 4, 10
chalk **8:** 10
charcoal **8:** 22–23, **11:** 26, **13:** 41
charge, furnace **4:** 24, 25
chemical bonds **8:** 7
Chernobyl **15:** 37
china clay **9:** 26, 28
chlorates **14:** 24
chloride ions **1:** 34, **2:** 9, 22, 26,
   14: 8, 20
chlorinated hydrocarbons **14:** 30
chlorination **14:** 11
chlorine (Cl) **See Vol. 14 and
   Vol. 16:** 11, 14, 40–41;
   1: 15, **2:** 7, 12, 23, 26, 27,
   6: 33, **8:** 33, **12:** 12,
   13: 20, 40
chloroethene **8:** 33, **14:** 23
chlorofluorocarbons **12:** 12,
   14: 38, 39

chloroform **14:** 5
chlorophyll **3:** 34
cholera **14:** 16
chromatography **7:** 35, **8:** 20
chrome **12:** 32
chrome alloys **4:** 36
chrome oxide **4:** 38
chrome steel **4:** 36
chromic acid **4:** 37
chromic oxide **4:** 37
chromite **4:** 36
chromium (Cr) **See Vol. 4 and
   Vol. 16:** 42; **9:** 29
chromium oxide **11:** 24, 25
chromium III oxide **4:** 39
cinnabar **6:** 5, 26
circuit **9:** 36, 37
citric acid **1:** 18, 30, 31
citrine **9:** 12
Cl *see* chlorine
clay **3:** 29, **7:** 7, 8, 34, 36, **9:** 26, 29
Cm *see* curium
CN gas **14:** 26
Co *see* cobalt
coal **8:** 7, 10, 13, **12:** 24, 38
cobalt (Co) **See Vol. 16:** 43;
   4: 34, 41, **9:** 7, 41
cobalt hydroxide **1:** 33
cobalt sulphide **13:** 24
cobalt-60 **15:** 17, 27, 43
coinage metals **5:** 4
coins **5:** 20, 28, 41
coke **1:** 24, **4:** 25, 27, **5:** 11, **10:** 10,
   12: 24, 26, 29, **13:** 27
collector **9:** 36
colour **3:** 8, 10
combustion **11:** 39, **12:** 34, 38,
   13: 14
compounds **2:** 5, 22, **3:** 4, 7, 41,
   4: 20, **8:** 7, **11:** 39, 41,
   12: 15, 35, 39, **13:** 15,
   16: 4, 11–13
Comstock Lode **5:** 30, 31
concentrated acid **1:** 19
conchoidal fracture **9:** 15
concrete **3:** 5, 23, **15:** 9, 35
condensation nuclei **14:** 8, 40
condensation polymers **8:** 36–37
conduction, electrical **2:** 22, 23,
   5: 16, **7:** 28, **12:** 9
conduction, heat **5:** 15, **7:** 29,
   30, 31
Contact process **13:** 28–29
control rods **15:** 34, 35
copper (Cu) **See Vol. 5 and Vol.
   16:** 11, 44–45; **1:** 12, 29,
   2: 23, **4:** 6, 7, 40, **6:** 8, 10,
   12, 20, 22, 37, **7:** 4, 22, 28,
   8: 17, **10:** 11, 15, 41, **11:** 5,
   30, 37, **12:** 25, 28, 29, **14:** 12
copper carbonate **5:** 6, 7, 26, 27,
   13: 34
copper chlorate **14:** 24
copper chloride **14:** 12
copper complex **5:** 27, **13:** 37
copper deficiency **5:** 22
copper hydroxide **1:** 33, **5:** 27
copper nitrate **5:** 14, 26, **11:** 31
copper ores **5:** 6–7, 10
copper oxide **5:** 8, 9, 11, 24, 26,
   8: 17, **12:** 23, 25
copper sulphate **1:** 25, **3:** 37, **4:** 6,
   7, **5:** 13, 23, 24, 26, **6:** 10, 12,
   12: 28, **13:** 32, 34–37, 42

copper sulphide **5:** 8, 11, 26, **12:**
   29, **13:** 12, 13
coral **3:** 4, 9, 10
corrosion **1:** 9, 26, 36, **3:** 13, 36,
   4: 6, 7, 8, 9, 10, 32, 35, 37,
   40, 41, **5:** 15, 21, **6:** 16,
   7: 14, 33, **10:** 38, **12:** 30, 32
corundum **7:** 6, 9, **12:** 11
cosmetics **10:** 30
cosmic radiation **15:** 10, 14, 15
covalent bond **1:** 11
Cr *see* chromium
cracking **1:** 14, 15, **8:** 26, 27
cross-linking **8:** 34
crude oil **1:** 14, 15, **8:** 24, 25,
   26, 27
cryogenics **1:** 41
cryolite **7:** 18
crystal **2:** 8, 9, 13, 22, 35, **9:** 10, 11,
   12, 13, 14, 15, 20, 21, 24, 25,
   28, 29, 37
crystals **3:** 8, **4:** 13, **5:** 24, **7:** 6, 16,
   8: 8–9, **13:** 10–11, 33, **14:** 8
Cs *see* cesium
CS gas **14:** 26
Cu *see* copper
cubic **9:** 20
cubic crystal **2:** 8, 9, 22, **4:** 18, 19,
   13: 12, 13, 15
cubic zirconia **9:** 21
curie **15:** 13, 22
Curie, Marie and Pierre **15:** 5,
   22, 23
curing **2:** 25
curium (Cm) **16:** 46
currency **5:** 41
current **9:** 34
cyanide **14:** 26
cyclotrimethylenetrinitramine
   11: 27
Czochralski method **9:** 35

D

Daniell cell **6:** 13
Daniell, John **6:** 12
Darby, Abraham **4:** 5
Db *see* dubnium
DDT **8:** 42, **14:** 29
decomposition **4:** 23, **10:** 20, 21,
   11: 25, 32, **14:** 7
decorative brass **5:** 19
decrepitation **11:** 32
deflagrating spoon **13:** 14
dehydrating agent **13:** 26
dehydration **1:** 24, **8:** 19
deionised **1:** 10
denitrifying bacteria **11:** 23
dental **14:** 5
desalination **2:** 14
desert roses **3:** 8, **13:** 13
detergent **2:** 37, 40, **3:** 40, **12:** 21,
   11: 43
deuterium **15:** 30, 38
deuterium-tritium fusion **15:** 30
dialysis **2:** 19
diamond **7:** 6, **8:** 8, **9:** 12, 13, 21,
   14: 37, **16:** 10
diaphragm (electrolysis) **2:** 26
diaphragm cell **1:** 14, **14:** 18, 20,
   21, 25
dichlorodiethyl sulphide **13:** 40
dichloromethane **14:** 31
die-casting **6:** 22
diesel **1:** 14, **8:** 26, 27

dilute acid **1:** 19
diode **9:** 34, 35, 37
dioxins **14:** 29
diphosphine **11:** 39
discharge tube **1:** 43, **2:** 38, 39
disinfectant **4:** 42, **11:** 12, **14:** 16, 43
displacement reaction **14:** 41
dissociate **1:** 11, 19, 30, 31, 32, **2:** 22
dissolve **2:** 25, **3:** 12
dissolving, aluminium **7:** 14–15
distillation **8:** 25
distilling nitrogen **11:** 8
DNA **1:** 8, 9
dolomite **3:** 5, 37, **10:** 7, **12:** 27
doping **9:** 35
Downs process **2:** 26, **14:** 19
dry ammonia **11:** 14
dry batteries (cell) **6:** 5, 14
dry cell **4:** 41
dry cleaning **14:** 30
dry ice **8:** 14
dry zinc–silver battery **6:** 13
dubnium (Db) **16:** 47
duralumin **7:** 23
Dy see dysprosium
dyes **1:** 24, **7:** 37
dynamite **11:** 13, 27, 28
dysprosium (Dy) **16:** 48

E

ebonite **13:** 38
einsteinium (Es) **16:** 49
ekaboron (Eb) see scandium
electrical cable **7:** 28
electrical conduction **2:** 23, 23
electrical conductor **5:** 16
electric arc process **4:** 30
electricity **9:** 34
electrode **3:** 37, **4:** 11, 41, **6:** 12, 13, **7:** 25
electrolysis **1:** 10, 11, 15, **2:** 23, 26–27, **4:** 11, 37, **5:** 12, 13, **6:** 9, **7:** 18, 19, **12:** 28, **14:** 19, 21, **16:** 14
electrolyte **1:** 31, **2:** 22, 23, **4:** 11, **6:** 12, 13, 14, 15, 33, **7:** 19, **10:** 29, **12:** 9, 18, **13:** 30, 31, **14:** 19
electrolytic cell **7:** 18, 19, 43
electron **1:** 36, 38, 39, **5:** 16, **6:** 10, 12, 13, **9:** 34, 35, **10:** 20, **15:** 6, 7, 8, **16:** 4, 11, 16
electron shell **14:** 6, **16:** 5
electronics **9:** 36
electroplating **4:** 37, **7:** 26
electrostatic precipitators **13:** 23
element **1–15:** 4, **16–18:** 4
    boiling point **16:** 16
    colour **16:** 15
    density **16:** 16
    melting point **16:** 16
    name **16:** 15
elemental, gases **16:** 11
elemental, state **16:** 4
elements
    origin of **15:** 7
    extraction from their
      compounds **16:** 14
    relative abundance **16:** 4
emerald **4:** 36, **9:** 12, 22, **12:** 10
emery **7:** 6
emitter **9:** 36

emulsion **4:** 38, **5:** 32, **14:** 43
enriched uranium **15:** 25, 33
environmental damage **11:** 43
environmental impact **8:** 42–43
Epsom salts **13:** 32
equations **1–15:** 46–47, **16–18:** 56–57
Er see erbium
erbium (Er) **16:** 50
Es see einsteinium
esters **1:** 30, **8:** 29, 41
ethane **8:** 28
ethanol **8:** 28
ethene **1:** 14, **8:** 27, 29, 32, 33, **13:** 40, **14:** 10, 22, 23
ethyl acetate **8:** 29
ethylene glycol **8:** 37, **12:** 36, 37
ethyl ethanoate **8:** 29, 31
ethyne **8:** 29
Eu see europium
europium (Eu) **16:** 51
evaporated **14:** 8
evaporation **2:** 11, 12, 13
exothermic **1:** 24, **14:** 12
exothermic reaction **2:** 34, 35, **12:** 14, 36
explosives **14:** 24, **11:** 24–29, 36
extrusion **7:** 20, 33

F

F see fluorine
fallout, nuclear **15:** 39
fast reactor core **15:** 33
fat **1:** 30, 32, **2:** 35, **8:** 29
Fe see iron
feldspar **2:** 8, 41, **7:** 7, 10, **9:** 10, 11, 26, 28
Fermi, Enrico **15:** 33
fermium (Fm) **16:** 52
ferric hydroxide **1:** 33, **4:** 14
ferric oxide **4:** 11
ferrocyanide **4:** 15
ferrous **4:** 14
ferrous hydroxide **4:** 15
fertiliser **1:** 16, 24, 26, **2:** 5, 40, **11:** 12, 13, 20–21, 36, **13:** 17, 29, 43
film badge **15:** 12
fire extinguishers **7:** 38, **8:** 15
fireworks **11:** 26
firing **9:** 28
fission **15:** 28–29, 34
fission bomb **15:** 38
fixing **5:** 32
fixing nitrogen **11:** 16–19
flame retardants **12:** 35
float glass **9:** 40–41
flocculate **3:** 25
flotation **5:** 10, 11
flowstone **3:** 14
fluorescence **14:** 9
fluorescent lights **6:** 35, 42
fluorescent tube **1:** 42, **2:** 38, 39
fluoride **14:** 4, 5, 37
fluorine (F) **See Vol. 14 and Vol. 16:** 53; **1:** 8, **8:** 33, **12:** 10
fluorite **14:** 9
fluoroethene **14:** 23
fluorspar **3:** 8, **14:** 36
flux **6:** 17, 25, **10:** 42, **14:** 36
Fm see fermium
food chain **6:** 39
fool's gold **4:** 18, **13:** 13
forged **4:** 28

formaldehyde **8:** 28
formalin **8:** 28
Fort Knox **5:** 41
fossil **3:** 11
fossil fuels **3:** 13, **8:** 11, 12, **13:** 5, 16
fossy jaw **11:** 38
Fr see francium
fractional distillation **11:** 8, 9, **12:** 17
fractionation **8:** 24–27
fractionation column **8:** 25, **11:** 8
fractionation tower **1:** 14, **8:** 26, 27
fractions **8:** 25, 26
francium (Fr) **17:** 4
Frasch process **13:** 16, 17
Frasch, Herman **13:** 16
freezing point, water **2:** 24
freon **14:** 38
froth flotation process **6:** 8, **10:** 11
fucus red **6:** 38
fuel **1:** 6, 7
fuel element **15:** 26
fuel rod **15:** 5, 33, 34, 35
fuming nitric acid **1:** 26, **6:** 28
fungicide **5:** 22, 23, **6:** 24, 25, **14:** 28
furnace **4:** 30
fused silica **9:** 38
fusion **1:** 6, 7, **15:** 30–31
fusion bomb **15:** 38

G

Ga see gallium
gadolinium (Gd) **17:** 5
galena **10:** 6, 7, 30, **13:** 12, 24
gallium (Ga) **17:** 6
gallium arsenide **6:** 42
galvanic cell **6:** 13
Galvani, Luigi **6:** 11, 16
galvanised iron **4:** 10
galvanising **6:** 16–17, **12:** 32, 33
gamma radiation **15:** 8, 9, 15, 42
gamma rays **15:** 8
gangue **5:** 11, **6:** 9, **10:** 11, 12
garnet **4:** 40, **9:** 20
garnetiferous mica-schist **9:** 20
gas **1:** 4
gas oil **1:** 14
gasoline **1:** 14, **8:** 26, 27, **10:** 4, 32
Gd see gadolinium
Ge see germanium
geiger counter (Geiger–Müller tube) **15:** 12, 13, 21
Geiger, Hans **15:** 12
gelatin **5:** 32
gelatinous precipitate **4:** 15, **13:** 36
gemstone **7:** 8, 9, **9:** 12, 13, **12:** 10
germanium (Ge) **17:** 7
geysers **3:** 17, **13:** 9
gilding metals **5:** 18
glass **2:** 30, 40, **3:** 22, **4:** 40, **9:** 15, 23, 30, 38, 40, 41, **10:** 26, 27
glass-ceramic **9:** 30
Glauber's salt **13:** 32, 33
glaze **4:** 38, **10:** 24, 25
global warming **8:** 12
glucinium see beryllium
glucose **5:** 34, **8:** 10, 11, 18, **12:** 15
glycerol **1:** 32, **2:** 35
glycerol trinitrate **8:** 6, **11:** 27
goiter **14:** 40

gold (Au) **See Vol. 5 and Vol. 17:** 8–9; **6:** 8, 37, 39, **9:** 16, **10:** 7, 11, **11:** 37
gold leaf **5:** 40
gold plating **5:** 43
gold rush **5:** 37, 38
Goodyear, Charles **8:** 35, **13:** 38
grains **9:** 21
granite **2:** 8, 41, **7:** 6, 10, **9:** 11, 20, 22, 23, **15:** 18, 23
graphite **7:** 19, **8:** 8, 9, 22, **14:** 18, 19, **16:** 10
green gold **5:** 42
Greenhouse Effect **7:** 41, **8:** 12, 42
greenhouse gas **7:** 40
green vitriol **13:** 32
groups (Periodic Table) **16:** 5, 8
    see also Periodic Table
Guinea **7:** 11
guncotton **11:** 27
gunpowder **2:** 41, **11:** 26, **13:** 40, 41
gypsum **3:** 8, 30, **11:** 43, **13:** 12, 13, 32

H

H see hydrogen
Ha (hahnium) see dubnium
Haber-Bosch process **1:** 16, 17, **11:** 16
haematite **4:** 12, 13, 15, **12:** 11
haemoglobin **12:** 15
hafnium (Hf) **17:** 10
hahnium (Ha) see dubnium
half-life **15:** 16–17, 18
halides **5:** 33, **14:** 8
halite **2:** 8, 9, **14:** 8, 9
Hall, Charles Martin **7:** 12
Hall–Héroult process **7:** 19
halogens **2:** 40, **8:** 23, **14:** 4, 5, 6, 22
halothane **14:** 5
hard water **3:** 38, 40
hassium (Hs) **17:** 11
He see helium
heart **2:** 41
heat conduction **5:** 15
heavy water **16:** 14
helium (He) **See Vol. 1 and Vol. 17:** 12; **15:** 25, 30, 42
Henckel, Johann **6:** 8
herbicides **8:** 42
Héroult, Paul L. T. **7:** 12
hexagonal crystal **9:** 10, 22
hexandioic acid **8:** 36
hexan-1,6-diamine **8:** 36, 38
hexan-dioyl chloride **8:** 38
Hf see hafnium
Hg see mercury
high-level waste **15:** 40
Hiroshima **15:** 38
Ho see holmium
Hoffman's Voltameter **1:** 10, 11, **12:** 18
holmium (Ho) **17:** 13
hornblende **9:** 24, 43
hot springs **3:** 17
Hs see hassium
Hs (wolfram) see tungsten
hydrated **13:** 35
hydrated, lime **3:** 24
hydrocarbons **8:** 6, 24–25, 29, **14:** 23

hydrochloric acid **1**: 12, 13, 18, 22–23, 28, 34, 35, **3**: 34, 43, **6**: 11, 28, **8**: 15, **11**: 36, **14**: 10, 11, 13, 15, 17, 22, 23, 32, 33, 34, 35
hydroelectric power **7**: 13
hydrofluoric acid **14**: 37
hydrogen (H) **See Vol. 1 and Vol. 16**: 14; **17**: 14–15, **2**: 6, 27, 42, **3**: 7, 34, **4**: 41, **8**: 6, **11**: 16, 17, 37, **12**: 8, 18, 19, 38, **13**: 26, **14**: 19, 21, 22, 32, **15**: 30, 38
hydrogen bomb **15**: 21
hydrogen bonding **1**: 8–9, 10, 11
hydrogen chloride **1**: 22, **14**: 13, 32, 33, 34
hydrogen fluoride **14**: 37
hydrogen gas **6**: 11
hydrogen ions **1**: 10, 20, 32, 34, 36, **12**: 9, 19
hydrogen peroxide **12**: 21
hydrogen sulphide **1**: 27, **2**: 33, **4**: 18, **5**: 29, 34, **6**: 40, **13**: 4, 10, 16, 24–25, 25, 37
hydrogen-3 (tritium) **15**: 17
hydrometer **13**: 31
hydrophilic **2**: 37
hydrophobic **2**: 37
hydrothermal deposits **5**: 36, **10**: 6
hydrothermal veins **5**: 30, **6**: 6
hydrothermal vents **13**: 8
hydrous **4**: 13
hydroxide ions **1**: 10, 11, 20, 32, 34, **3**: 25, 29, **12**: 9
hypochlorous acid **14**: 17

I

I *see* iodine
ice **1**: 8
ice, prevention **2**: 24
Iceland Spar **3**: 8
igneous rock **9**: 11, 18, 20, 21, 23, 25, **15**: 18
In *see* indium
incandescent lights **1**: 42, 43, **11**: 11
incendiary device **11**: 40
indicator **1**: 21, 35, **2**: 6, 7, **4**: 6, **11**: 15, **12**: 18
indium (In) **17**: 16
induction period **12**: 36, 37
inert **1**: 39
inert gas **1**: 36, 38
infrared radiation **10**: 20
inner transition metals *see* **16**: 8 Periodic Table
inorganic chemicals **8**: 5, **16**: 13
insoluble **1**: 32
insulator **9**: 34
intermediate level waste **15**: 40
internal combustion engine **8**: 16, **12**: 40
iodine (I) **See Vol. 14 and Vol. 17**: 17
iodine-131 **15**: 43
ion **1**: 11, 34, 36, **2**: 22, 23, 27, **3**: 29, 41, **4**: 19, 23, **6**: 13, **11**: 43, **15**: 12, **1–15**: 47, **16–18**: 57
ionisation **15**: 12
ionise **12**: 9
ionised **1**: 11
ions **7**: 18, **9**: 26, 38

Ir *see* iridium
iridium (Ir) **See Vol. 17**: 18; **5**: 28
iron (Fe) **See Vol. 4 and Vol. 17**: 19–20; **1**: 26, **3**: 36, **6**: 16, **7**: 24, **9**: 29, 41, 43, **10**: 38, 39, **11**. 17, **12**: 26, 27, 30, 34
iron chloride **4**: 14, 15
iron filings **4**: 7
iron foundry **4**: 29
iron hydroxide **4**: 11, 14, 15, **12**: 31
iron ore **4**: 13, 17, 22, 25, 27
iron oxide **7**: 16, **8**: 17, **9**: 13, 18, 19, **11**: 42, **12**: 11, 23, 26, 32, 34
iron oxides **4**: 11, 12, 13, 14, 15, 16, 22, 24, 27, 30, 40
iron sulphate **4**: 7, 15, **13**: 15, 32
iron sulphide **4**: 18, 19, 21, **13**: 15, 24
iron III compounds **4**: 14
iron III hydroxide **1**: 33, **4**: 11, 14
iron II compounds **4**: 14
iron II hydroxide **4**: 15
irradiation **15**: 42–43
irrigation **2**: 20, 21
isoprene **8**: 35
isotope **11**: 6, **15**: 4, 7

J

jade **9**: 12, 24
Jamaica **7**: 11
jasper **9**: 13
jet engines **9**: 30
jewellery **5**: 28, 40, **8**: 8
junction diode **9**: 34, 35

K

K *see* potassium
kaolinite **7**: 7, **9**: 26, 28, 29
karst **3**: 11
Kellner, Karl **2**: 26
kerosene **1**: 14, **8**: 26, 27, **12**: 38
key facts, explanation **16**: 15
kidneys **2**: 19, 41
kiln **9**: 28, 29
KLEA **14**: 39
knocking **10**: 32
Kr *see* krypton
Krugerrand **5**: 41
krypton (Kr) **See Vol. 1 and Vol. 17**: 21
krypton-92 **15**: 28
kyanite **9**: 21

L

La *see* lanthanum
lampblack **8**: 22
lanthanides, lanthanide series **16**: 8 *see also* Periodic Table
lanthanum (La) **17**: 22
laterite **4**: 17, **7**: 11
latex **8**: 34
lather **3**: 38
lattice **5**: 16
lava **3**: 8, **9**: 11, 15, 21, 23, 25
Lawes, John **13**: 43
lawrencium (Lr) **17**: 23
lead (Pb) **See Vol. 10 and Vol. 17**: 24–25; **6**: 8, 21, **13**: 30, **15**: 9, 10, 11
lead-acid battery **6**: 13, **10**: 28, 29, **13**: 30–31

lead carbonate **10**: 7, 24
lead chamber process **10**: 17
lead chromate **4**: 39
lead dioxide **10**: 18, 28, 29, **12**: 22, **13**: 30
lead IV oxide **10**: 18
leaded fuel **10**: 32
leaded glass **10**: 23
lead flashing **10**: 23
lead hydroxide **10**: 31
lead in fuels **10**: 32
lead monoxide **10**: 8, 10, 18, 21, **12**: 22
lead nitrate **4**: 39, **10**: 20, 21, **11**: 32, 33, **13**: 24
lead oxide **10**: 18, 26, 27, 28, 29
lead pipes **10**: 22
lead poisoning **10**: 14, 31
lead shot **10**: 14, 15
lead silicate **10**: 24
lead sulphate **10**: 7, 16, 24, 28, 29, **13**: 32
lead sulphide **10**: 7, 10, 13, 30, **13**: 12, 24
lead II oxide **10**: 8, 18
Leblanc, Nicolas **2**: 28
Leclanché cell **6**: 14
Leclanché, Georges **6**: 14
legumes **11**: 18
Les Baux **7**: 11
leukemia **15**: 23, 27
Li *see* lithium
Liberty Bell **5**: 21
light **14**: 7
light-emitting diode (LED) **9**: 34, 35
lighthouse **6**: 31
lightning **11**: 6, 7, 22
lignin **8**: 18
lime **1**: 32, **2**: 29, **3**: 22, 24, **4**: 30, **7**: 16, **11**: 14, **13**: 34, 42
lime glass **9**: 38, 39
limescale **3**: 16, 38
limestone **1**: 29, 34, **2**: 28, 29, **3**: 4, 10, 12, 19, 20, **4**: 24, 26, 31, **8**: 10, **9**: 38, **10**: 7, **12**: 26
limestone rock **14**: 35
limewater **3**: 7, 26
limonite **4**: 13, 15
liquified petroleum gas (LPG) **8**: 27
liquid air **12**: 17
liquid crystal display (LCD) **9**: 37
liquid nitrogen **11**: 8, 9
litharge **10**: 8, 18
lithium (Li) **17**: 26
litmus **1**: 21, **14**: 15
litmus paper **1**: 20
lode **5**: 30, 36, **10**: 34, 35
lodestone **4**: 12
low-level waste **15**: 41
Lr *see* lawrencium
Lu *see* lutetium
lubricating oil **1**: 14
lutetium (Lu) **17**: 27

M

Macintosh, Charles **8**: 35
magma **5**: 30, **6**: 6, **9**: 16, 21, 23, 25, 29, 43, **10**: 6, 34
magma chamber **9**: 43
magnesium (Mg) **See Vol. 3 and Vol. 17**: 28–29; **1**: 18, 36, **4**: 6, 22, **6**: 22, **7**: 25, **9**: 26, **11**: 37, **12**: 33

magnesium carbonate **3**: 37, 43
magnesium hydroxide **1**: 32, **3**: 42, 43
magnesium ions **3**: 34, 40
magnesium oxide **3**: 37
magnesium ribbon **3**: 34, 37
magnesium silicate **9**: 27
magnesium sulphate **13**: 32
magnetic flea **4**: 39
magnetic properties **4**: 20
magnetite **4**: 12
malachite **5**: 7
mallee **2**: 17
manganese (Mn) **See Vol. 4 and Vol. 17**: 30; **7**: 22, **9**: 20, 29, 41, 43
manganese carbonate **4**: 42
manganese chloride **14**: 11
manganese dioxide **6**: 15
manganese nodules **4**: 41
manganese oxide **4**: 40, 41, 43
manganese sulphate **4**: 42
manganese sulphide **4**: 40
mangrove **2**: 16, 17
manure **11**: 20
marble **3**: 4, 18
Marram grass **2**: 17
massicot **10**: 18, **12**: 22
matches **11**: 38, 40, 41, **14**: 25
Md *see* mendelevium
medicines **13**: 42
meitnerium (Mt) **17**: 31
membrane **2**: 15, 27
"memory" brass **5**: 19
Mendeleev, Dmitri Ivanovich **16**: 5, 6, **17**: 7, 32, **18**: 11, 17
mendelevium (Md) **17**: 32
meniscus **6**: 30
mercuric chloride **6**: 32
mercuric chromate **6**: 29
mercuric nitrate **6**: 28, 29
mercuric oxide **6**: 32
mercuric sulphide **6**: 38
mercurochrome **6**: 32, 38
mercurous chloride **6**: 32
mercury (Hg) **See Vol. 6 and Vol. 17**: 33–34; **1**: 37, **5**: 35, 42, **7**: 22, **11**: 37, **14**: 18
mercury amalgam **14**: 19
mercury battery **6**: 32
mercury cathode cell **6**: 33, **14**: 18, 19
mercury cell **6**: 15, 33
mercury poisoning **6**: 38
mercury vapour lamps **6**: 34
metalloids **16**: 8 *see also* Periodic Table
metal oxides **1**: 32
metals **1**: 12, 32, 36, **2**: 6, 42, **3**: 6, **9**: 20, 26, 34, **16**: 8 *see also* Periodic Table
metamorphic rock **9**: 20, 23, 24
meteorites **4**: 12
methane **8**: 6, 24, 28
methanol **1**: 4
methyl benzene **13**: 10, **14**: 7
methyl group **9**: 32
methylmercury **6**: 39
methyl orange **1**: 21, 35
Mg *see* magnesium
mica **7**: 7, **9**: 26
microchip **9**: 37
microcrystalline **9**: 14
micronutrient **5**: 22

microorganisms **14:** 16
microprocessors **9:** 36
mild steel **4:** 32, 33, 34
Milk of Magnesia **3:** 42
mineral **2:** 9, **3:** 8, 15 , **8:** 8, **9:** 9, 11, 12, 20, 21, 43 , **12:** 10, **13:** 12–13
mineral acid **1:** 18, 19, 24, 25, **13:** 26, 27
mining **2:** 12, **5:** 10, 30, 36, 38, **7:** 10–11, **10:** 6, 7, 12, 34, 36
mirrors **5:** 34, 5
mixtures **4:** 20, **16:** 4, 12
Mn *see* manganese
Mo *see* molybdenum
molecule **2:** 19, 27, **9:** 11, **12:** 9, **13:** 6
molybdenum (Mo) **See Vol. 17:** 35; **4:** 34, **13:** 12
monoclinic crystal **13:** 10, 11, 13
monomer **13:** 38, 39, **8:** 32, 33
monoxide gas **10:** 10
mordant **7:** 36
mortar **3:** 22
MOSFETs (metal oxide semiconductor field effect transistors) **9:** 36
Mt *see* meitnerium
mullite **9:** 29
murex **14:** 42
muriatic acid **14:** 34
muscles **2:** 41
muscovite **7:** 6, **9:** 26, 27
mustard gas **13:** 40, **14:** 26

N

N *see* nitrogen
Na *see* sodium
Nagasaki **15:** 38, 39
nail-polish **8:** 29, 31
nail-polish remover **8:** 29, 31
naphtha **1:** 14
napping **9:** 14
native copper **5:** 7
native elements **16:** 10
native gold **5:** 36
native metal **4:** 12, 13
native silver **5:** 30
natural gas **8:** 10, 13, 24
Nb *see* niobium
Nd *see* neodymium
negative terminal **6:** 14
Ne *see* neon
neodymium (Nd) **17:** 36
neon (Ne) **See Vol.1 and Vol. 17:** 37
"neon" lights **2:** 39, **17:** 37
neon tubes **1:** 40
neptunium (Np) **17:** 38
nerve cells **2:** 18
neutral **1:** 20, 34
neutralisation **1:** 34–35, **2:** 31, 33
neutralise **3:** 21, 25, 43
neutron radiation **15:** 8, 9
neutrons **15:** 7, 8, 28, **16:** 4, 5
Ni *see* nickel
nickel (Ni) **See Vol. 17:** 39; **4:** 34, 36, 41, **5:** 40, **7:** 22
nickel–cadmium cell **6:** 41
nickel sulphide **13:** 12, 25
nielsborhium (Ns) *see* dubnium
Nightingale, Florence **14:** 16
niobium (Nb) **17:** 40
niobium-101 **15:** 29

nitrate fertiliser **11:** 20
nitrates **11:** 20
nitric acid **1:** 18, 22–26, 27, 37, **5:** 14, 26, **6:** 28, **7:** 33, **11:** 5, 6, 7, 13, 30, 33, 36–37
nitric acid, fuming **5:** 14
nitric oxide **1:** 26, **10:** 17, **11:** 7, 34, 35, 37, **12:** 42, 43
nitrifying bacteria **11:** 23
nitrocellulose **11:** 27
nitrogen (N) **See Vol. 11 and Vol. 17:** 41–42
nitrogen **1:** 8, 16, 17, 42, **8:** 6, 36, **12:** 17, **15:** 10
nitrogen cycle **11:** 22–23
nitrogen dioxide **1:** 26, 37, **6:** 28, **10:** 17, 21, **11:** 5, 7, 30–33, 34, 35, 37, **12:** 13, 41, 42, 43
nitrogen-fixing bacteria **11:** 18
nitrogen-fixing nodules **11:** 19
nitrogen oxides **7:** 40, 43
nitroglycerin **8:** 6, **11:** 27
nitrous oxide **11:** 34
No *see* nobelium
Nobel, Alfred **11:** 27
nobelium (No) **17:** 43
noble gases **1:** 5, 38–39, **11:** 8, **16:** 11
noble metals **5:** 28, **6:** 28
non-metals **16:** 8 *see also* Periodic Table
non-stick **14:** 37
Novocaine **14:** 5
NO$_x$ **11:** 34–35
Np *see* neptunium
Ns (nielsborhium) *see* dubnium
n-type region **9:** 34
nuclear accidents **15:** 36–37
nuclear energy (nuclear power) **1:** 6, **15:** 32–33
nuclear fusion **1:** 6
nuclear power station **15:** 32
nuclear reactions **15:** 4, 7
nuclear reactors **15:** 34–35
nuclear waste **15:** 40
nuclear weapons **15:** 38
nucleus **15:** 4, 6, 7, 8
nugget **5:** 36, 37
nutrients **2:** 16, 18, 20
nylon **8:** 31, 36, 37, 38, 39

O

O *see* oxygen
obsidian **9:** 15
ochre **4:** 15
octane **1:** 14
octane numbers **10:** 32
Oersted, Hans Christian **7:** 12
oil **8:** 10, 13
oils **1:** 30
oil spill **8:** 42
oil-storage tanks **3:** 37
olivine **9:** 21, 27
oolitic limestone **3:** 10
opal **9:** 14
oral rehydration **2:** 18
ore **3:** 10, **4:** 13, 17, 18, 24, 27, 36, **5:** 8, **6:** 6, 8, **7:** 10, 11, 13, **10:** 6, 8, 10, 34, 35, 36, **13:** 12, 15
ore-flotation **5:** 11
organic acid **1:** 18, 19, 30, 31, **2:** 30, **3:** 39
organic chemicals **8:** 5, 20, 42, 43

organic compounds **8:** 28, **16:** 13
organic solvents **14:** 7
organochloride **14:** 28, 29
Os *see* osmium
oscillator **9:** 37
osmium (Os) **17:** 44
osmosis **2:** 14–15, 16, 17, 19, 25
oxalic acid **1:** 30
oxidation **3:** 35, **4:** 11, 13, 23, 27, 31, **6:** 14, **8:** 10, 11, 18, **9:** 29, **12:** 6, 14, 24, 25, 26, 34, 36, **14:** 11, 14, 15, 16
oxide **4:** 8, 9, 17, **7:** 7, 8, 14, 24, 26, 33, 34, 35, **10:** 8, **12:** 10, 22, 30
oxidisation **10:** 11
oxidise **4:** 8, 16, 27, 30, 31, 40, **13:** 20
oxidising agent **4:** 42, 43, **6:** 28, **11:** 30, **12:** 20, 37
oxyacetylene **12:** 16, 39
oxygen (O) **See Vol. 12 and Vol. 17:** 45–47; **1:** 8, 10, 11, **2:** 43, **4:** 9, 11, 12, 14, 16, 22, 23, 30, 40, 41, **7:** 6, 38, 39, **8:** 10, 11, 18, 28, **9:** 9, 10, 26, 33, 38, **11:** 7, 9, 33, 35, **13:** 14, **14:** 24, 25
oxygen cycle **12:** 14
oxygen, test for the presence **17:** 47
ozone **11:** 35, **12:** 6, 12, 13, 42, 43, **14:** 38, 39
ozone layer **14:** 38

P

P *see* phosphorus
Pa *see* protactinium
painkillers **14:** 5
paint **6:** 19, **10:** 24, 25, **12:** 21, 32
paint stripper **14:** 31
palladium (Pd) **See Vol. 17:** 48; **5:** 28, **12:** 41
panning **5:** 39
paraquat **14:** 29
Parkes, Alexander **8:** 31
Parkes process **10:** 10, 11
patina **1:** 29, **5:** 4, 6, 27
Pb *see* lead
PBB *see* polybrominated biphenyls
PCBs *see* polychlorinated biphenyls
Pd *see* palladium
pearl **3:** 4
pentaerythrite tetranitrate **11:** 27
perchloric acid **12:** 39
percolate **3:** 14, 15
Periodic Law **16:** 5
Periodic Table **1–15:** 44–45, **16:** 4, 5, 6–7, 8, 54–55, **17–18:** 54–55
periods (Periodic Table) **16:** 5 *see also* Periodic Table
permanent hardness **3:** 38
pesticide **2:** 30, **6:** 24, 25, **8:** 42, **13:** 42, **14:** 28, 29
Pete Bog **15:** 18
PETN **11:** 27
petrochemical plant **8:** 26, 29
petrochemicals **8:** 26
petroleum **8:** 7, 24, **14:** 22
Pewter **10:** 40
pH **1:** 20, 21, 28
phenolphthalein **1:** 21, **2:** 6, 7, **11:** 15
phosgene **14:** 26

phosphates **11:** 42
phosphine gas **11:** 39
phosphor **6:** 35, 42, 43
phosphor bronze **5:** 20
phosphoric acid **10:** 24, **11:** 42, **12:** 32
phosphorus (P) **See Vol. 11 and Vol. 17:** 49–50; **3:** 40, **5:** 20, **9:** 34, **10:** 41
phosphorus oxide **11:** 39
phosphorus, red **14:** 25
photochemical smog **12:** 42
photoelectric cell **6:** 5, 42, 43
photoelectric properties **10:** 20
photographer's hypo **5:** 33, **13:** 33, **14:** 43
photographic films **8:** 41
photography **5:** 32, **14:** 42, 43
photon **6:** 43
photosynthesis **8:** 10, 11, **12:** 6, 14
photovoltaic cell **6:** 42
pickling **2:** 25
piezoelectric effect **9:** 37
pig iron **4:** 24, 27, 28, 30
pigment **4:** 38, **6:** 24, 40
pitchblende **15:** 22, 24
placer deposit **5:** 39, **10:** 36
plaster **3:** 5, 31
Plaster of Paris **3:** 31, **13:** 12, 32
plastic **8:** 30–31, 43
plastic, properties **8:** 30
plastics **14:** 22, 23
plastic sulphur **13:** 7
platinum (Pt) **See Vol. 17:** 51; **5:** 28, **10:** 33, **11:** 37, **12:** 41, **14:** 20
playa lakes **14:** 8, 9
playas **2:** 10
plumbing **10:** 22
plutonium (Pu) **See Vol. 17:** 52; **15:** 26, 34, 35, 38
Pm *see* promethium
Po *see* polonium
poison **6:** 32, **11:** 38
poison gas **14:** 26
pollutants **7:** 42, **14:** 16
pollute **11:** 20
pollution **2:** 20–21, 33, **3:** 13, **10:** 12, **12:** 40, 42, **13:** 18, 19, 22, 23, **15:** 20
polonium (Po) **See Vol. 17:** 53; **15:** 23,
polonium-210 **15:** 17
polybrominated biphenyls **14:** 29
polychlorinated biphenyls **14:** 28
polychloroethene **8:** 33, **14:** 10, 22, 23
polyester **8:** 31, 36, 37, 40, 41
polyethene **8:** 31, 32, **14:** 23
polyfluoroethene **14:** 22, 23
polymer **2:** 26, **9:** 33, **13:** 38, 39, **14:** 23, 36
polymerisation **8:** 32–39, **13:** 39, **14:** 22, **9:** 4, 32
polymers **8:** 30–41
polystyrene **8:** 31, 33
polytetrafluoroethene **8:** 31, 33, **14:** 36, 37
polyvinyl benzene **8:** 33
polyvinyl chloride **8:** 33, *see also* polychloroethene
polyvinyl fluoride *see* polyfluoroethene
porous **3:** 10, **4:** 9

porous bronze **5:** 20
Portland cement **3:** 23
positive terminal **6:** 14
potash **2:** 40
potash salts **2:** 41
potassium (K) **See Vol. 2 and Vol. 18:** 4–5; **4:** 6, **7:** 6, **9:** 11, 26
potassium carbonate **2:** 40
potassium chlorate **11:** 41, **14:** 24, 25
potassium chloride **6:** 13, **14:** 11
potassium chromate **4:** 38, 39, **6:** 29
potassium dichromate **4:** 38
potassium-40 **15:** 11
potassium hydroxide **2:** 42, **4:** 43, **6:** 15
potassium iodide **14:** 41
potassium manganate **4:** 42, 43, **14:** 15
potassium metal **2:** 42
potassium nitrate **1:** 27, **2:** 40, 41, 42, 43, **4:** 42, 43, **11:** 4, 21, 26, 36, **13:** 41
potassium nitrite **2:** 43
potassium permanganate **4:** 42, 43, **12:** 21, 36, 37, **14:** 10
potassium phosphate **2:** 40
potassium sulphate **2:** 40
pottery **9:** 28
power stations **13:** 22
Pr *see* praseodymium
praseodymium (Pr) **18:** 6
precious metal **5:** 28, **10:** 16
precipitate **3:** 7, 16, 26, 38, **4:** 39, 41, **13:** 23, 36, 37
precipitation **3:** 14, **14:** 8
preservatives **13:** 42
preserving **2:** 25
primary dry battery **6:** 15
printed circuits **5:** 17
procaine hydrochloride **14:** 5
promethium (Pm) **18:** 7
protactinium (Pa) **18:** 8
protein chain **8:** 36
proteins **8:** 10, 18, 36, **11:** 4
proton number **16:** 5
protons **15:** 7, 8, **16:** 4, 5
prussian blue **4:** 15
Pt *see* platinum
PTFE **8:** 33
p-type region **9:** 34
Pu *see* plutonium
PVC **8:** 33 *see also* polychloroethene
PVF *see* polyfluoroethene
pyrite **4:** 18, 19, 21, **10:** 17, **13:** 12, 13, 15, 16, 24
pyrolusite **4:** 41
pyroxenes **9:** 24

Q

quartz **4:** 18, **9:** 10, 11, 12, 13, 14, 15, 18, 26, 37, 38, **12:** 10
quartzite **9:** 16
quicklime **3:** 20, 22, 24
quicksilver **6:** 26

R

Ra *see* radium
radium (Ra) **18:** 9
radiated **7:** 30
radiation **1:** 7, **10:** 26, 31, **15:** 8, 42, 43

radiation sickness **15:** 42
radiation therapy **15:** 43
radioactive decay **15:** 16
radioactive decay, graph **15:** 16
radioactive elements **15:** 4, 6, 26–27, **16:** 8
radioactive isotopes **1:** 42
radioactive tracers **15:** 20–21
radioactivity **15:** 5, 7, 8–9
radioisotopes **15:** 17
radium **1:** 43, **15:** 5, 15, 17, 22–23, 36
radon (Rn) **See Vol. 1 and Vol. 18:** 10; **15:** 14, 23, **16:** 10, 23
Ramsay, Sir William **1:** 38
rate of chemical reaction **2:** 24
Ravenscroft **10:** 22
rayon **8:** 38
Rb *see* rubidium
RDX **11:** 27, 28
Re *see* rhenium
reaction **3:** 6
reactivity **2:** 7, 42, **4:** 7, **5:** 15, 29, 41, **6:** 16, **7:** 6, 14, 24–25, **10:** 16, **11:** 10, **14:** 5, 6, 41
reactivity series **1:** 36, **2:** 7, **3:** 36, **4:** 6, 40, 41, **5:** 15, 29, 41, **6:** 11, 16, **7:** 24, **10:** 16, 39, **12:** 28
recycling **7:** 40
red gold **5:** 42
red lead **10:** 18, 24, **12:** 22
red mud **7:** 17, 42
red mud pollution **7:** 42
red phosphorus **11:** 38, 40–41
redox reaction **12:** 24, 25
reduced **4:** 24, **10:** 8
reducing **14:** 14
reducing agent **4:** 25, 27, **5:** 8, 34, **8:** 16, 17, **13:** 20, 24
reduction **4:** 11, 23, **5:** 8, 9, **7:** 18, **12:** 24, 25, 26, **13:** 20
refining **5:** 12, 31, 39, **6:** 9, 37, **7:** 12, 18–19, **12:** 28, 29
refining metals **1:** 4
reflection **7:** 30
refrigerants **14:** 38, 39
refrigeration **11:** 12
refrigerator **14:** 38, 39
Reims cathedral **3:** 13
reinforced concrete **4:** 32
relative atomic mass **16:** 7
rem (roentgen equivalent in man) **15:** 43
reprocessing, uranium **15:** 25
resin **3:** 41, **12:** 20
resistors **9:** 37
respiration **8:** 10, **12:** 14
reverse osmosis **2:** 14
Rf *see* rutherfordium
Rh *see* rhodium
rhenium (Re) **18:** 11
Rhizobium **11:** 18
rhodium (Rh) **See Vol. 18:** 12; **5:** 42
rhombic crystal **13:** 5, 10, 11
rhombohedral-shaped crystal **3:** 9
rings **9:** 22
riveting **4:** 28
Rn *see* radon
rocks **9:** 12
rock salt **2:** 8, 10, 12, **14:** 8, 9, 19
Romans **10:** 30
Ru *see* ruthenium

rubber **8:** 34, 35, **9:** 33, **13:** 38
rubidium (Rb) **18:** 13
ruby **4:** 36, **7:** 8, 9, **9:** 13, 22, **12:** 11
rust **4:** 7, 8–11, 35, **7:** 24, **10:** 38, 39, **12:** 30, 32
rust-inhibitor **11:** 42
ruthenium (Ru) **18:** 14
Rutherford, Ernest **15:** 9
rutherfordium (Rf) **18:** 15

S

S *see* sulphur
sacrificial anode **6:** 18, **7:** 25
salicylic acid **1:** 30
saline **2:** 11, 20, **14:** 9
saline drip **2:** 18
saline solution **2:** 9, 18, 19
salinisation **2:** 20, 21
salt **1:** 22, 32, 33, 34, **2:** 6, 7, 8–17, 18, 21, 24, 26, 28, 40, **13:** 9, **14:** 8, 9, 19, 34
salt bridge **6:** 13, 14
saltbush **2:** 17
salt deposits **2:** 8
salt dome **2:** 12, **14:** 19, **13:** 8
salt pans **2:** 12, 13, 40
saltpetre **11:** 4, 21, **13:** 41
salt pollution **2:** 20
salts **2:** 40, 41, 42
samarium (Sm) **18:** 16
sand **9:** 38, 40
sand dunes **9:** 19
sandstones **9:** 18
saponification **2:** 34, 36, 37
sapphire **7:** 8, 9, **12:** 10
saturated **3:** 6, 7
Sb *see* antimony
Sc *see* scandium
scale **3:** 10, 39
scandium (Sc) **18:** 17
schist **9:** 20
scrubbing **2:** 33, **13:** 17
scum **3:** 40
Se *see* selenium
seaborgium (Sg) **18:** 18
sea-salt **2:** 13
sea water **2:** 13, **14:** 4, 9, 40, 42
seaweed **14:** 4, 9, 40
secondary battery **6:** 13, **13:** 31
sediment **9:** 18, 21
sedimentary rocks **9:** 18
sediments **2:** 10
selenide **9:** 41
selenium (Se) **See Vol. 18:** 19; **6:** 42
semiconductor **6:** 43, **9:** 34, 35
semi-metals *see* metalloids
semipermeable membrane **1:** 15, **2:** 14, 15, 16, 25, **6:** 14, 15
serpentine **9:** 27
sewage systems **14:** 16
Sg *see* seaborgium
shales **7:** 36
shell diagrams **16:** 4, 5
sheet minerals **7:** 7
sheet silicate **9:** 27, 29
Si *see* silicon
silica **4:** 26, **9:** 9, 10, 14, 16, 29, 35, 38, 39, 42, 43, **10:** 26, **11:** 38, **12:** 10
silicate **4:** 40, **9:** 8, 9, 11, 12, 18, 20, 26
silicate groups **9:** 9

silicates **12:** 10
silicon (Si) **See Vol. 9 and Vol. 18:** 20–21; **4:** 29, 30, 34, **6:** 42, **7:** 6, 22, **10:** 41, **12:** 10
silicon bronze **5:** 21
silicon carbide **8:** 5, **9:** 30
silicon chip **9:** 4, 34
silicone **9:** 32, 33
silicon wafer **1:** 42, **9:** 34
silver (Ag) **See Vol. 5 and Vol. 18:** 22–23; **6:** 8, 37, **7:** 31, **10:** 7, 11, **13:** 33
silver bromide **5:** 32, 33, **14:** 42, 43
silver chloride **5:** 32, 33, **14:** 7
silver chloride battery **6:** 15
silvering **5:** 34
silver iodide **5:** 32, 33, **14:** 40, 43
silver oxide battery **6:** 15
silver rush **5:** 30
silver salts **5:** 32
silver sulphide **5:** 29, **13:** 25
sink holes **3:** 12
sinter **3:** 17
sintering **9:** 29
slag **4:** 24, 26, 27, 30, 40, **10:** 10, **12:** 26
slaked lime **3:** 24, 28, **11:** 14
sluice box **5:** 38, **10:** 36
Sm *see* samarium
smelling salts **11:** 12
smelter **7:** 13, 18
smelting **4:** 24–27, **5:** 11, **6:** 8
smithsonite **6:** 6
smog **11:** 34, **12:** 41, 42, **13:** 22
smoke detectors **15:** 15
smoky quartz **9:** 12, 13
Sn *see* tin
soap **1:** 30, 32, **2:** 34, 35, 36–37
soda **2:** 4, 30
soda ash **2:** 29, 30, **7:** 16
soda glass **9:** 39
soda lakes **2:** 41
soda-lime glass **9:** 38
sodium (Na) **See Vol. 2 and Vol. 18:** 24–25; **1:** 36, **7:** 6, **9:** 11, 24, 38
sodium aluminate **2:** 32, **7:** 15, 17
sodium azide **11:** 29
sodium bicarbonate **2:** 28, 29, 30–31, **8:** 14
sodium carbonate **2:** 28–29, 30–31, **7:** 38, **8:** 15, **9:** 39, 40
sodium chlorate **14:** 14, 24, 25
sodium chloride **1:** 32, **2:** 6, 7, 8, 9, 12, 13, 23, 24, 27, 29, 31, **4:** 14, **6:** 33, **9:** 13, **13:** 9, **14:** 4, 8, 9, 19, 25
sodium hydroxide **1:** 30, 32, 34, 35, **2:** 6, 26, 27, 30, 32–35, 36, **4:** 14, 15, **5:** 27, **6:** 33, 41, **7:** 14, 15, 16, **13:** 23, 25, **14:** 14, 19, 20, 21
sodium ion **1:** 34, **2:** 9, 22, **3:** 40, **14:** 8, 20
sodium metal **2:** 6, 7
sodium pellet **2:** 6
sodium peroxydisulphate **13:** 20
sodium, radioactive **15:** 20
sodium stearate **2:** 36
sodium sulphate **13:** 32, 33
sodium sulphide **2:** 33
sodium sulphite **13:** 20
sodium thiosulphate **5:** 33, **13:** 33, **14:** 43

sodium triphosphate **11:** 43
sodium vapour lamps **2:** 4
soil **3:** 12, 24, 28, **4:** 16–17, **7:** 43
soil conditioner **3:** 24, 28
solar cell **6:** 42, **9:** 35
solder **10:** 42, 43
soldered **7:** 20
solder glasses **10:** 27
Soliman's Water **6:** 38
soluble **1:** 32, **9:** 38
solution **2:** 23, 34, **3:** 12, 16, 27, **4:** 7, 15, 17, **7:** 15, 17, **9:** 13, 15
solution mining **2:** 12
Solvay, Ernest **2:** 28
Solvay process **2:** 28–29, 32
solvent **8:** 28, 29, 31, **14:** 7, 30
soot **8:** 22, **14:** 13
SO$_X$ **13:** 22
space suits **7:** 30
spectrum **1:** 38
sphalerite **4:** 18, **6:** 6, **13:** 12
spontaneous combustion **11:** 39, **12:** 36, 37
stable **9:** 10
stainless steel **4:** 34, 35, 36
stalactite **3:** 14
stalagmite **3:** 14, 39
starches **8:** 43
stars **1:** 6–7, **15:** 31
state **1–15:** 46, **16–18:** 56
stationary phase **7:** 35
steam **3:** 24
steel **1:** 22, **4:** 30–35, **6:** 18, **7:** 21, 25, 33, **10:** 38, **12:** 32
steel furnace **12:** 25
steelmaking **12:** 26
sterling silver **5:** 28
stomach **1:** 28
Stone Age **9:** 14
stratosphere **12:** 12
striations **4:** 18, **9:** 23
strong acid **1:** 18, 19, 20, **13:** 18, 19, 26
strong alkali **1:** 20
strontium (Sr) **18:** 26
strontium chlorate **14:** 24
strontium-90 **15:** 27, 39, 42
strontium-94 **15:** 29
styrene **8:** 33, 35
styrofoam **8:** 33
Sr *see* strontium
sublimation **8:** 14, 15
sucrose **1:** 24, **8:** 19
sugar **1:** 24, **8:** 10, 19
sugars **12:** 14
sulphates **13:** 12, 32–33, 43
sulphide **10:** 8
sulphides **5:** 6, **13:** 8, 12, 16
sulphites **13:** 18, 32–33, 42
sulphur (S) **See Vol. 13 and Vol. 18:** 27–28; **4:** 19, 20, 21, 30, 40, **8:** 34, 35, **10:** 10, 12, **11:** 26
sulphur bridge **13:** 39
sulphur dioxide **2:** 33, **4:** 10, **6:** 8, 9, **10:** 10, 12, 17, **12:** 13, 29, **13:** 5, 9, 14, 16, 18–23, 28
sulphur, flowers **13:** 7
sulphuric acid **1:** 18, 24–25, 27, 37, **2:** 33, **4:** 18, 19, 42, **6:** 28, **7:** 36, **8:** 19, **10:** 10, 16, 17, 28, 29, **11:** 36, 42, 43, **13:** 16, 18, 26–31, 34, 43

sulphuric acid, dilute **5:** 24
sulphurous acid **13:** 18, 19
sulphur oxides **7:** 40, 43
sulphur trioxide **13:** 19, 28, 29
Sun **1:** 6, **15:** 30
supernova **15:** 31
superphosphates **1:** 24, **11:** 42, 43
superphosphate fertilisers **13:** 29
suspension **4:** 38, **13:** 17
swarf **4:** 7
swimming pool **14:** 16, 17
swimming pool disinfectant **14:** 43
switch **6:** 30
symbols, chemical **1–15:** 46–47, **16:** 4, 15, **16–18:** 2, 56–57
synthetic fibre **8:** 38–41
synthetic ivory **8:** 31

T

Ta *see* tantalum
table salt **14:** 4, 9
talc **9:** 26
tantalum (Ta) **18:** 29
tarnish **5:** 29
tarnishing **13:** 25
tartaric acid **1:** 18, 30, **8:** 14
Tb *see* terbium
Tc *see* technetium
Te *see* tellurium
tear gas **14:** 26
technetium (Tc) **See Vol. 18:** 30; **15:** 20
teeth **3:** 5, 33, **14:** 37
Teflon **8:** 31, 33, **14:** 36
telluride **10:** 20, **18:** 31
tellurium (Te) **18:** 31
temperature, effect of salt **2:** 24
tempering **4:** 33
temporary hardness **3:** 38
terbium (Tb) **18:** 32
terephthalic acid **8:** 37
tetraethyl lead **10:** 32
tetrafluoroethene **8:** 33, **14:** 36, 37
tetrahedron **8:** 8, **9:** 9, 10, **12:** 10
tetraphosphorus trisulphide **11:** 41
Th *see* thorium
thallium (Tl) **18:** 33
thermometer **6:** 31
thermoplastic **8:** 33, **14:** 22
thorium (Th) **18:** 34
thoron **15:** 14
Three Mile Island **15:** 36
thulium (Tm) **18:** 35
Ti *see* titanium
tiger's-eye **9:** 13
tin (Sn) **See Vol. 10 and Vol. 18:** 36–37; **3:** 36, **5:** 18, 20, **6:** 37, **7:** 4, **9:** 16, 40, **12:** 32, 33
tin can **7:** 33
tincture of iodine **14:** 40
tin dioxide **10:** 35
tin oxide **10:** 34, 35, 36
tin plating **10:** 38, 39, **12:** 33
titanium (Ti) **See Vol. 18:** 38; **7:** 22, **9:** 30, 31, **14:** 20
titration **1:** 34, 35
Tl *see* thallium
Tm *see* thulium
TNT **8:** 6, **11:** 13, 27
topaz **12:** 10
Torricelli, Evangelista **6:** 30
tourmaline **9:** 22, 23

transistor **9:** 36, 37
transition elements **16:** 8 *see also* Periodic Table
translucent **9:** 11
transmutation **15:** 10
travertine **3:** 8, 14, 16
trichloroethene **14:** 30
trinitrotoluene **8:** 6, **11:** 27
tripod **4:** 43
tritium **15:** 8, 17, 21, 30, 38, **17:** 14
tungsten (W) **See Vol. 18:** 39; **4:** 34
tungsten steel **4:** 35
turbines **7:** 23
turpentine **14:** 30

U

U *see* uranium
ultraviolet light **6:** 35, **8:** 30, 33, **12:** 12, **14:** 39
Une (unnilennium) *see* meitnerium
Unh (unnilhexium) *see* seaborgium
Universal Indicator **1:** 20, **12:** 18
unleaded fuel **10:** 33
unnilennium (Une) *see* meitnerium
unnilhexium (Unh) *see* seaborgium
unniloctium (Uno) *see* hassium
unnilpentium (Unp) *see* dubnium
Uno (unniloctium) *see* hassium
Unp (unnilpentium) *see* dubnium
unsaturated hydrocarbons **8:** 29
ununbium (Uub) **18:** 40
ununhexium (Uuh) **18:** 41
ununnilium (Uun) **18:** 42
ununoctium (Uuo) **18:** 43
ununquadium (Uuq) **18:** 44
unununium (Uuu) **18:** 45
u-PVC **8:** 33
uranium (U) **See Vol. 15 and Vol. 18:** 46
uranium fission **15:** 28–29
uranium hexafluoride **14:** 36
uranium oxide **15:** 34
uranium-235 **15:** 28, 29
uranium-238 **15:** 11, 17
urea **11:** 13, 23
Uub *see* ununbium
Uuh *see* ununhexium
Uun *see* ununnilium
Uuo *see* ununoctium
Uuq *see* ununquadium
Uuu *see* unununium

V

V *see* vanadium
vanadium (V) **See Vol. 18:** 47; **4:** 34, **12:** 22
vanadium pentoxide **13:** 28
vapour **2:** 38
veins **4:** 18, **5:** 6, 30, 36, **9:** 16
Venus **13:** 9
vermiculite **9:** 26
vinegar **1:** 31
vinyl **8:** 33, **14:** 22
vinyl chloride **8:** 33; *see also* chloroethene
vinyl fluoride *see* fluoroethene
viscous **9:** 43
vitreous **2:** 9
Volta, Alessandro **6:** 12
Voltage **9:** 34
von Liebig, Justus **5:** 34
vulcanisation **8:** 34, 35, **13:** 38–39

W

W *see* tungsten
wafer **9:** 37
wallboard **3:** 30
washing **3:** 40
waste glass **9:** 40
water **1:** 9, 10–11, 28, **2:** 6–7, 10, 14, 15, 18, 22, 25, 30, 31, 34, 35, 42, **3:** 38, 40, **4:** 10, 11, 18, **8:** 36, **9:** 14, 26, 28, 29, **12:** 4, 8, 9, 14, 15, 18, 19, 38
water of crystallization **13:** 35
water supplies **14:** 16
water-softener **3:** 40
waterproof **9:** 33
weak **1:** 29, 31
weak acid **1:** 19, 20, **13:** 18, 19
weak alkali **1:** 20
weather **1:** 29
weathering **3:** 12, 19, **9:** 18, 19, 20, 21
weedkillers **14:** 24, 29
welding **12:** 39
wet batteries **13:** 30
white gold **5:** 42
white lead **10:** 24, 30
white phosphorus **11:** 38–39
whitewash **3:** 23
wolfram (Hs) *see* tungsten
World War I **8:** 31, **13:** 40, **14:** 26
World War II **15:** 38
wrought bronze **5:** 20
wrought iron **4:** 28, 29

X

Xe *see* xenon
xenon (Xe) **See Vol. 1 and Vol. 18:** 48; **15:** 20
xenon-140 **15:** 29
X-rays **10:** 26, 31, **15:** 8, 14, 15, 36

Y

Y *see* yttrium
Yb *see* ytterbium
ytterbium (Yb) **18:** 49
yttrium (Y) **18:** 50

Z

zinc (Zn) **See Vol. 6 and Vol. 18:** 51–52; **1:** 12, 37, **4:** 10, 41, **5:** 18, **7:** 25, **10:** 7, 11, **12:** 32, 33, **13:** 8, 26, **14:** 32
zinc–cadmium battery **6:** 13
zinc carbonate **6:** 6, 7
zinc cell **6:** 12, 15
zinc chloride **6:** 17, 25
zinc hydroxide **6:** 41
zinc oxide **6:** 9, 24
zinc sulphate **6:** 9, 12, 25
zinc sulphide **4:** 18, **6:** 6, 9, 25, **13:** 12
zircon **9:** 20, 21
zirconium (Zr) **See Vol. 18:** 53; **9:** 12, 21
Zn *see* zinc
Zr *see* zirconium